Julia Stevens

Like Him

Tree of Life Publishing

Cover Design by Esther
Formatted by Angela Selfe
Front Cover Artwork by Nicole-Shiffers
Printed in the UK

Dedication

To the King of my heart, Jesus of Nazareth.
Make me more like You.

Acknowledgement

Thanks to my husband Matt for your detailed eye, continual support, generosity and love. To David for your expert help publishing, editing and proof-reading. To Mum, Grace, Paula, Ralph and Simone for taking the time out to edit and encourage. And finally, to Nicole for your stunning painting.

Endorsements

Julia Steven's book is intimate and character building as it weaves in and out of her own life's experiences.

These add vibrance to the truths she painstakingly uncovers to share with us.

We all wish to exhibit our Heavenly Family's DNA. We all wish to be like him. Julia Stevens helps us to move in that direction.

This book is warm and loving.

Anna Rountree,
Author, 'Heaven Awaits The Bride'

Julia is a seer, a woman of character and integrity, a generous-hearted joyful giver, a wonderful mother, wife and leader and I've been privileged to call her my best friend since childhood. In her book she shares many life-changing encounters she's had with the Lord and how truths revealed in His word have transformed her into His image. I pray that as you read the pages of this book, you'll have similar encounters with Jesus, and receive fresh manna from His word, in the process becoming more like Him.

Paula O'Keefe,
Missionary to Russia and Spain, Living Waters

"Like Him" enables our focus to be drawn to our desires for Christ, prayer, and our own need of being broken, humble, accountable and available to God's Spirit. Through Julia's fresh scriptural in-sight she reveals how far we can stray from what God regards as normal church life. From a personal perspective, I was really impacted by the chapter called Ruling and Reigning in His Love, things opened up to me which were life changing and a delight.

This book will hopefully play a key part on bringing us to God's dynamic norm for His people.

John Larkin
Restoration House Church & Kingdom Connections Family

Contents

Introduction

HAVE YOU HAD A MOMENT in a day when you suddenly realised that you are doing well? A moment when you felt that you were living up to your hopes for yourself in terms of behaviour, feelings, and positive self-perception? In that moment, you are aware of being more 'you' than usual.

This little book is about extending those moments into hours, days and years, so that by the Holy Spirit you eventually become whole and complete. Perhaps those flashes are the real you, when you are fully aligned with your Father in heaven and with how He sees you.

I wrote this book for you as an encouragement – to remind you who you really are; to give insight and revelation; to enable you better to live in the revelation that the more you know God, the more you know yourself. To be able to live more fully in Him. I have written these pages from a realisation that you and I are on a journey of finding our true identity. Though many of us have not yet arrived, we can gain deeper realisation each day as we read His Word about who we are in Jesus, and about the assignment from heaven that Father God has for us. I trust this book will be a part of your process of transformation into His likeness and that the process will be accelerated as a result.

I have included short prayers, poems and diagrams to help you in this journey. I have explained some of the Hebraic meaning behind the English translations of the Bible in order to deepen your revelation and understanding.

The more you know the living Word, the more you know who you are.

And we all by raising the veil are transformed from glory to glory just as by the Spirit of the Lord, to behold for one's self the glory of the Lord.

(2 Corinthians 3:18)

Let us agree together that you would know *'what is the height, breadth, and depth of the love of God'* for you and that you know that you cannot be separated from His love as you live in Him. I pray that as you read, you will have more revelation of who you are. Surrender your life to Saviour again today. You are everything God's Word says you are.

Setting the Scene

During 2018, due to a sudden awareness that I did not fully realise or understand my true identity in God in some areas of my life, I began writing these words. I was asked by a wonderful man of God called John Tolo, to be part of planning, leading, and gathering people to pray for the United Kingdom to know revival and specifically for a large outreach event in London.

In the context of leading gatherings into prayer, I felt surprised and inadequate at the suggestion that I could lead in this way. I had felt unsure whether people would gather together or how to draw the people to pray. However, in stepping out, I found Jesus helping me to move more into my true identity and in hindsight I learnt that Father God had a plan, which He orchestrated very well.

When we move out of our places of comfort we are often not prepared. Faith in God is a must and our Father is with us and will both enable and encourage us. We grow as we step out of our comfort zones.

On a sunny Tuesday afternoon, at a church in Guildford, United Kingdom, a lady whom I had met a few days before told me "I have been carrying this around the world for a while, asking Father God who to give it to. He says you are to have it!" I looked down at what was in her hand; it was a golden key chain pendant about three inches long, in the shape of a kind of sceptre. It had a crown on the top and was dotted with tiny diamanté gems. The little key at the foot of it was in the shape of a heart.

As she gave it to me, I was immediately reminded of a visitation I had from an angel in 2005, which brought a commissioning for me from heaven. The angel gave me a spiritual golden sceptre into my hands and gave me a scripture to go with it from Isaiah 11, which I write about later in this book. The angel also delivered me a message with the sceptre: that I am 'a priest of the Most High God'. All at the same time, I had a realisation that I did not fully know who I was in terms of my identity in God. We can sometimes struggle in knowing who we are even if all of heaven is on our side! This struggle sent me on a heart search to be more established in my identity in Father God.

Sharon Thorburn, who gave me the pendant, had also been carrying other amazing spiritual items around the world in her travels. Included was a torch of hope and a song she composed with the help of Holy Spirit called 'Light a Candle'. She had prophetically been singing this song over every nation. Sharon is a composer from New Zealand with a calling to travel the nations bringing prophetic declaration of God's love and calling to go out and share the gospel of Jesus to the nations.

Our house was full at the first prayer meeting as I stepped into the role of leading people in intercession. Together we lit the torch of hope Sharon had been carrying. We lit it as a prophetic sign of 'The Light of the World' shining in our land and of all the souls who would be saved. As the torch was lit, Sharon sang the spiritual song she had been given by God. It was such a special gathering to pray specifically for people to become believers in the Lord Jesus. It was the first of many prayer meetings for a big outreach event in London called 'Power and Love'. We went on to have monthly meetings to pray for this huge interactive street ministry outreach. What a marvellous Father we serve who always gives us the encouragement we need and helps gather us together to pray.

I often wear the lovely pendant I was given as a reminder about who I am in God. Since receiving it I have heard of men and women who have been given keys and necklaces as a sign from Father God. There was the lady on our prayer team who had a similar experience as she was sent on outreach to Africa and there was the young lady at our outreach who was given a pendant by a pastor after giving her life to Jesus. Whilst attending 'Awaken The Dawn UK' in 2018, the prophet Chuck Pierce also gave out several keys to men and women in Wembley after giving a key prophetic word over the United Kingdom. I believe this is an encouraging sign that the bride of Jesus is arising and being equipped with keys of His kingdom to bring about His will on earth.

Another important meaning of this receiving of gifts is that they are a love gift from Father God and from Jesus, our bridegroom, before the great and glorious wedding ceremony takes place at the end of the age; the marriage of Jesus with His bride. I am part of this beautiful bride and I pray that you are also.

Father God knows that some of us need reminders now and again of who He has made us to be. The words in this book are to help grow and encourage you in your identity in Him. One of these days we shall arrive, be fully whole, knowing who we truly are, beside our King in heavenly realms; in the meantime, I trust that some of the following heart-words may help you along the way.

The key chain given to me is an emblem of power and love, being a royal sceptre as well as a key with a heart-shaped tuning fork. Father God had orchestrated this gift as part of the encouragement I needed to know more about who I am in Him, and to provide confirmation and encouragement to me in my involvement in prayer and intercession ministry. I encourage you today, to take every invitation which is from your Father in heaven, even if you think you are not adequate. He has chosen you and will give you what you need to accomplish His growth in your life. You are His and He has great plans for you!

Ask our Father in heaven what and who He has called you to be and do. I know for sure that Father made you wonderfully and has a good and hopeful plan for your life. Let us agree together that your life on earth is aligned with the destiny book our Father has for you in heaven. Our Father will continue to bring you and I signs of love and encouragement as we journey into becoming who we truly are. I pray that you would clearly hear what the Father is calling you to in these days and that as you step out you would continually be full of all boldness, confidence and the love of the Lord.

We are all part of the body of Jesus our Saviour and although you and I may not always agree on every aspect of theology, we can be in unity under His headship. Perhaps at times you may think that some of the experiences I have written about are extreme, however, I can assure you that they happened just as I relate and there are evidences and witnesses to back many of them.

Here is one example of such a revelation.

One night I had a vision of the open tomb after Jesus had risen. In the vision, Mary came out of the darkness of the tomb and into the light. She saw a man nearby and assumed he was the gardener. She asked him where the body of Jesus was. As soon as Jesus called her name: 'Mary' there was a moment of huge revelation – a realisation of the risen Lord Himself! Everything in Mary's life changed at the moment she saw her risen Lord. Jesus had not yet ascended at this time to the right hand of His Father in heaven.

Father God showed me that some of the followers of Jesus in these days have not seen Him clearly. They may have seen him as the risen Lord, but not as risen, ascended and reigning in their own lives.

However, He is calling out their names, for each one to realise He is their master teacher who wants to show them who they really are, in terms of their eternal walk. He wants to show them the depth of the revelation of His resurrection, ascension and ruling authority. He calls each one of us by name to be more like Him and walk by faith, deeper into revelation of His death, resurrection and who He is as ascended Lord over all things. The more we know Him, the more we know the authority we have in Him.

On the instruction of Jesus, Mary, went and told the other followers of Jesus that He was to ascend to His Father. Jesus is calling us to show those who believe that their ascended Saviour, who delivers them from chaos and destruction, is risen *and ascended*! We can fully know Him *and ourselves* in this heavenly risen reality. We are a risen creation, a brand-new people due to all Jesus has achieved for us all.

Jesus is your risen Lord, seated at the right hand of your Father on high and He wants you to know you are seated in heavenly places next to Him (Ephesians 2:6). Spiritually speaking, Jesus has given you authority to rule and reign in His righteousness in this life and the next. Jesus called Mary by name. He has called you by name, you are His. When you realise and have faith that He is the ascended King of your whole life, and that you rule and reign with Him, you are then enabled to walk more in the greater works He has for you.

Within these pages are details of several angelic visitations. Many angelic experiences occur in Scripture, some of these are: Mary met an angel after Jesus' resurrection (Matthew 28); Abraham and Hagar were visited by and heard angels (Genesis 16, Genesis 22); Jacob contended with the Angel of the Lord; Joshua was given strategy by an angel for battle; Mary and the shepherds were visited by angels who bought good news of Jesus birth; an angel spoke to Philip about the way to go (Acts 8); and an angel spoke to Cornelius and Peter about their meeting before it occurred.

These messengers bring God's very words to His people and they happen because our Father God wants to speak with you and empower His beloved children by His Word and Spirit. Discerning these angelic spirits is also a key. We are to test them to see if the words they speak line up with the Word of God. We can also use our senses; if they emit love and peace they will be from God's throne; if the opposite, they are from an enemy of God. I have read many books on this subject and would recommend such writers as Paul Keith Davis, Gary Oates and John Paul Jackson.

I hope that which I have encountered and some of things revealed to me by reading God's Word and listening to God's Spirit will help you on your journey to knowing who you are in Him. I have tested the revelations I have had with the Word of God in Scripture and I encourage you to do the same. Holy Spirit always talks to us in a way that is consistent with the Word of God and revelation is written that we might have more faith.

The experiences within these pages are prophetic, the blessing from the impartation of the Word of God and Holy Spirit journey that I have experienced so far, is available for you to receive. I pray that you are able to receive prophetic inspiration and higher insight as you read this book, and that the words would be like a breath of Holy Spirit air to you.

ONE

Where I've Been

VOICE OF FREEDOM
(AN EARLY POEM)

There is a storm within my soul
My mind is clouded, shrouded
With misty thoughts of fear and woe
But even so, from deep down inside
I hear a voice cry out from the turmoil of my mind
My Lord's words are bold and clear
Full of love to cast out the fear
As Father speaks the storm is stilled
My soul with everlasting hope is filled
Unguarded thoughts are made to cease
Taken captive by the Prince of peace
In full surrender my soul responds
My mind concentrates, meditates
With thoughts good and right
O God of might, I rejoice with all the saints
For you bring life and strength to the soul which faints

I WAS EIGHTEEN YEARS OLD and was looking for adventure so I travelled to the land of Israel. I know now that I was led by Father God, but at the time I thought it was simply to better myself.

As a young girl I was very shy, and even more so as a teen. Due to my fair complexion, I turned red easily, and I found it extremely difficult to speak among a group of my peers in a social setting, during my teens and early twenties.

I developed OCD (obsessive-compulsive disorder), and for many years if I was with a group of friends, I was not able to easily drink in public. This was due to anxiety inside concerning making a noise by swallowing! At the root of all anxiety is an irrational lie, quite often unknowingly received.

I hid the OCD quite well on the outside, but inside I was very stressed and anxious. Sensitivity concerning the feelings of others around me and their 'perceptions' of me was overwhelming during those years, and I felt negative about myself quite a bit. It was an ordeal for me to be out in groups of others, but inside, half of me wanted to join in the fun, so I continued pushing forward. I took part in church youth groups as much as I could, though I felt that I was one 'looking on' and rarely joined in conversation while in group situations. I so wanted to join in and be a part of the team, but my emotional state at the time did not always allow me to do so. I have learnt that it is important to be kind to one another as there are many still suffering with this type of anxiety.

In my mind, going to Israel to live in a community would remedy this situation. My thinking was that it would force me to be with groups of people, and therefore I would have to speak up. I envisaged returning home a changed person full of confidence. Reality is often a little different from our expectations!

My seven months at Immanuel House (Beit Immanuel) messianic Christian community in Jaffa, living with volunteers from all over the world, was full of adventure, and I felt a little more accepted and somewhat 'healed' of some elements of anxiety. However, being one of the quieter ones, I was given the post of laundry-maid, which meant that I spent most of my day on the roof pegging out wet laundry by myself, rather than working with others.

Being free from the fear of man has been a process over the years, and nowadays I can truly say that Father God, through the healing love of Jesus, has delivered me from this burden of fear, and I no longer have debilitating OCD. I have been freed from the fear of man, and I have since found that God has made me greatly sensitive for a reason. I am learning to receive Holy Spirits' help and submit to Him when I encounter overwhelming emotions.

Working on the roof in Israel became a blessing, and one of the highlights of my stay was to witness 'The Miracle of The Sheets'. On Easter Sunday in 1986, we travelled to Jerusalem by coach to join in the Garden Tomb Easter worship service with our church's ministry team to Jews. I rose at 5am to peg out forty or so sheets on the roof to dry.

Later, at the service, I remember us all huddled under umbrellas as it rained down heavily and we sang out our worship to God. I made a swift prayer: 'O Lord, keep my sheets dry!' On returning to Immanuel House, I immediately ran up the flights of stairs to the roof to find it covered in puddles, with hailstones filling the roof's edges and corners. To my amazement, each of the many sheets were bone dry! I ran around excitedly shouting down to our manager, "Brigette! Brigette! They're dry! God kept all the sheets dry for me!" How wonderful is our Father, who cares about the little things that matter so much to us all.

One of the main aspects of learning for me in Israel was a growing fondness for the Hebrew language and for the Israeli or Jewish lifestyle. I loved singing the beautiful messianic songs in Hebrew during our powerful multiracial gatherings, in which Jewish and Arab Christians gathered to worship together.

'A'hava to gdola-a, Kidaam, Yeshua niche pach' – this is the first line of a lullaby I was to sing to both my children twenty years later. *A'hava* means 'love' in Hebrew, and one of the root meanings to this word is 'to reveal the love of Abba Father'.[1] When we choose to love each other, we are revealing the Father's great love for each other. God is love.'

One of the people who had an impact on my life during that time was Dr Richard Wurmbrand who visited the House during our stay. He spoke to us of his time in prison, of sharing the good news of Jesus and of how he forgave his captors of their incessant torture.[2] The forgiving love of Jesus exuded from Dr Wurmbrand in a way I had never experienced before. I literally felt the love of Father God flowing out from him when he hugged me. I will never forget his embrace. Since then I often have visions of embracing Father God and Him embracing me. The embracing love of Father God heals you.

A fondness for all things Israeli and Hebraic has been part of the tapestry of my life ever since those seven months I spent at Beit Immanuel (in Hebrew this means 'The House Where God Is with Us'). In the pages of this book I mention the Hebrew meaning of certain words. I pray that you remember the root meanings behind the names and words when you read the Scriptures, this enables a deeper connection with the Spirit of the Lord. Knowing the root meaning of the original words is a revelatory treasure.

One of the meanings for the Hebrew words translated as 'I Am' (the revealed name of God) is 'I am being'. This name describes His ongoing reality of being outside of time itself. The 'I Am' keeps going continually, and forever was and will be. One needs much more than one sentence to describe some of the reality in the meaning of Hebrew words. I have found that to know the Hebrew meaning unlocks many jewels of revelation.

One of my best friends, Katy came with me to Israel, and she and I had wonderful adventures bicycling around the Lake of Galilee, visiting the eternal city of Jerusalem, and steeping ourselves in the messianic culture of *Shabbat*, Jewish weddings, and community living.

I have always been a thinker of all things spiritual from an early age, becoming an evangelistic eight-year-old when I gave my heart and life to Jesus. This was perhaps due to my mother having a dramatic conversion experience. She had been on depressants, with suicidal tendencies and she was being monitored by the local surgery. One day our neighbour Eileen came over. She shared with Mum about who Jesus is, and said to her: 'If you give your life to Jesus, He will give His life to you'. Eileen took Mum to a larger than life lady called Pam Robertson who prayed as she knelt in surrender, giving her life to God. Mum encountered God's power that day and received a flood of love from above. It was a gift of Faith.

I watched Mum rapidly and dramatically change her habits, from sad and difficult to happy and light-hearted. Eileen befriended Mum, and she was also knitted into a new church family at Fleet Christian Fellowship. Mum found the support system she had always longed for in the little church, which was the result of a revival in Chard, Somerset, UK.

The effect on me was impactful; I had evidenced something good, something phenomenal which had healed my mother. I, too, surrendered my life to Jesus in a children's meeting with Joanna O'Keefe, my best friend's mother. My family were all baptized in water in the summer of 1976, and I was filled with the Holy Spirit in the same year.

Throughout the years my faith has mainly grown by listening to God's guidance through reading His Word and experiencing Holy Spirit through visions and visitation. In more recent years, my relationship with Father God and my beloved Jesus has become closer as I experienced an outpouring of Holy Spirit joy in 1995; saw an open vision of Jesus in early 2000s; and had the visitation from an angel in 2005 commissioning me as a priest of the Most High.

From 2007, for three and a half years, I was mentored by a wonderful lady, Molly Sutherland, a local minister who went to Fuller Seminary in the United States under John Wimber. Molly is very special in that she was a practicing Catholic nun for six years, then worshipped as a practicing Protestant, and is now a non-denominational minister. I attended her small group ministry sessions with Resurrected Life Ministries, which are positively life-impacting as anyone who has attended them will know. During these sessions, I received and saw deliverance for the individual soul and experienced more fully, true unity within the corporate body of Jesus. My reliance on Father God and my relationship with Him have deepened greatly since.

There's a Messianic Torah Community locally that I sometimes frequent, which has also been life-changing for me. We learn the whole of the Scriptures as they are unfolded by a rabbi. He acts like a chairman and asks the whole group (a dozen or more people) questions about the passages we read concerning our head and heart knowledge of the Torah (the Bible's first five books). We read the scripture in context of Yeshua (Jesus) as our messiah. I have found that this way of teaching brings wonderful revelation, as I learn with the Holy Spirit, the messianic rabbi, and others. This ancient way of learning has endlessly deepened my walk with Father God.

I would like to give glory to Father God, who has freed me from OCD and from fear of man. Today, I am able to sing with the worship group at my local church; give testimony of God's goodness in front of whole groups of people; and to run a small business with my wonderful husband Matt, with all that that entails. This book is based on what I have learned from His Word and Spirit. I am sure there are many more layers to come and treasures to uncover. I encourage you to reflect on your journey so far and see where Father God has intervened and healed you along the way.

Perhaps you too had problems with anxiety. I have a scripture to help you overcome the anxiety and fear with which the enemy tries to deceive us. Please meditate on this verse:

> *'Surrender your anxiety! Says Jesus, be silent and stop your striving and you will see that I am God. I am the God above all the nations and I will be exalted throughout the whole earth . . . the mighty Lord of the angel armies is on our side!'*

(Psalm 46:1011 TPT)

Prayer of release

You are the Lord of love, Jesus our Saviour. We thank You for suffering so that we can be free from all fear and trauma.

In Your mighty authority, Lord Jesus, we tell the spirit of fear, anxiety, and torment to leave our bodies, our minds, and our emotions right now. We release by faith from heaven Your love, which we receive right now from You, Lord. We receive Your beautiful outpouring of love into our bodies, minds, and emotions.

Thank You, Holy Spirit for helping us to walk in love and not fear.

Amen

(If you do not yet fully know Jesus your Saviour as the way, truth, and life, please read Chapter 12 next.)

1. Hebrew Word Pictures, Frank T Seekins
2. Tortured for Christ' Richard Wurmbrand, 2004, Hodder & Stoughton.

TWO

The I AM – I Am Like Him

KNOWING

Knowing Him,
Him Knowing.
I am in I AM.
In I AM, I am.
I will stay in Him,
He will stay in Me
Eternally.

Knowing Him,
Him Knowing.
You are in I AM
In I AM, you are.
You will stay in Him,
He will stay in you.
The 'I will be' in you Eternally.

FATHER GOD is forever loving and before major shifts take place he always speaks to His children in many ways, including through His prophets.

When Moses heard God, it caused a major shift in history. Moses encountered God in the wilderness and asked who He was, God replied; *'I AM WHO I AM'* (Exodus 3:14 NKJV). God then gave Moses a mission to go and save the enslaved nation he belonged to. God said, 'Tell the people 'I AM' sent you'.

'I AM' is one of the most powerful and mysterious names of God. I believe this name of God is linked to who *we* are when we come into the fullness of dwelling in Him: the 'I AM-ness' of God in us. The 'I AM' is in us when we surrender our lives to Him.

When you see the words 'I am' in the English language, in the bible and in worship songs, listen to the Holy Spirit, as these words are a living connection directly to God and who He is. When you submit to the fullness of who He has made you, you are being one with the I AM-ness of God. I have found this a great help in connecting with The Lord.

In Hebrew the name of God: 'I AM' is huge. It means 'I was; I will be who I will be'. God is sovereign and is outside of our time. He is present, He was, and He will be. He is your glorious creator God and you are His creation made in His likeness. When we are fully in His presence we are in His kingdom, in His 'I will be'. This is where we can know Him and His plans for us individually and corporately.

Since learning more about His name and meditating on Him, I have had a quickening inside my spirit, an activation of the knowledge of Holy Spirit about God's name. Many times, when I hear the words 'I Am', I literally feel them resonating deeply inside myself. My whole body also tingles in worship when I sing the words 'I am' in identification with The I AM. It gives me a surety of truth that I am not only made by Him, but I am now made new and I am more fully like Him every day. I truly am a new creation, a brand-new person.

This gives me an ongoing sense that all is well. It gives me an ability to more fully live in His rest and comfort. By the same token, I can now hear more clearly when I (or someone else) say something that is out of line with the truth of who God is and of all that I am in Him and He is in me. I pray that you and I would have an increasing revelation of the truth of the mystery of His name. The I AM is in you when you are saved.

Faith in *the* 'I AM' and His Word is key to knowing who He is and therefore who we are in Him. Let us often remember and declare who we really are from His Word:

> *I am one in Messiah Jesus: 'So that all would be one, just as You, Father, are in Me and I in You, that they also would be in Us . . . that they would be one just as We are One'*

(John 17:2123)

> *I am in Messiah Jesus: 'Because of Him you are in Messiah Yeshua, who became wisdom from God in us, righteousness and also holiness and redemption'*

(1 Corinthians 1:30)

> *I am a light in the world: 'You are the light of the world. A city laid out on a mountain is not able to be hidden'*

(Matthew 5:14)

> *I am God's workmanship: 'we are His workmanship, as we have been created in Messsiah Yeshua for good works, which God prepared before-hand . . . so that we would walk in them.'*

(Ephesians 2:10)

I encourage you to make your own personal list to declare. For some months, my children and I would speak these types of declarations over ourselves, choosing a different few each day. It has given us confidence. Knowing His Word enables you to more fully walk into who you really are in Him.

Listening to the I AM is also a key. Join with me as we humble ourselves under His mighty hand daily, and listen to Him wherever we are, where the 'I AM' speaks to your core spirit.

Moses heard God's voice clearly when he was at work one day tending his father in law's flock on the far side of the wilderness (wilderness in Hebrew means 'the place of speaking'). The Lord God called out to Moses from a flame of fire within a bush. As he turned aside in this 'place of speaking' he encountered the Lord God of the universe. God revealed His very identity to Moses and unfolded plans for his future. Moses listened, humbled himself, obeyed and communicated with God, who revealed His goodness and promised to go with him. In becoming friends with God, Moses found his identity as leader of a nation.

Moses went up onto the mountain called 'Horeb' that day. 'Horeb' means desolation and dryness.[1]

Teachers such as Shawn Stone relate that Moses went up on this mount of 'desolation' in order to be honest with God and talk intentionally to Him; to repent and seek mercy concerning the murder he had previously committed in Egypt.[2]

I have learnt that the murder represents Moses independent attempt to 'save' his Hebrew brothers using human strength instead of reliance on God. This is a lesson to us. Moses had it in his heart to save his Hebrew brothers but let his emotions overwhelm him in this case, causing death. He did not take his thoughts and feelings to God but acted on impulse. Let us not let frustrations build up and try in our own strength to 'fix' things, to 'save' in our own way, but let us listen to our Father God in heaven about His ways, His right word on the matter, His plans for us. He desires to talk and walk with you, to have a deep relationship with you. Our Father has the best plan and solutions on any situation. The Father's heart is to save, to forgive and heal you and He has provided The Way through His son Jesus.

So here Moses was tending sheep on Horeb, mountain of dryness and desolation thinking about His past. At times we have all found ourselves in such a place; but be encouraged if you happen there, be honest with God like Moses, seek the Lord, seek His right word and action on the matter. For it was in this dry place, on a desolate mountain where Moses discovered who God was, and about his calling. Talk to Father God about the pain of the past and present, confess any disobedience, He is compassionate and quick to forgive. God loves to turn even the worst disobedience around. Father God has mercy to forgive you, through the saving grace of Jesus. Like with Moses, He wants to share with you the plan He has for your life, to prosper you, not to condemn you.

It had been forty years since he had fled from his palatial life in Egypt, and Moses was doing well in some ways. Through his act of lovingkindness, due to watering a strangers' animals, he had been accepted by a Midianite family and found a wife and home. His father-in-law, Jethro, had another name, Reuel, which means 'friend of God'. God had led Moses, who was later known as a 'friend of God', into the arms of a good family. Whilst living this relatively good life away from a whole other life, God drew Moses to turn aside to remember and gave him the plan to redeem himself to his birth family.

Like Moses, your life may be going well in this season; at times, you might struggle with things from your past or present trials. You may even be in a dry place in your relationship with God. The Lord is waiting for you to turn to Him, to be aware of His goodness toward you. He desires to speak with you as you seek and listen with your whole heart. He has redeemed you and brought you into His family, His Kingdom, where you always belonged. It says in His word:

> *'Lord, you've gone into my future to prepare the way,*
> *and in kindness, you follow behind me to spare me*
> *from the harm of my past,'*

(Psalm 139:5 TPT)

If you lack a sense of 'belonging' in some areas in your life, turn your heart towards Father God right now, in faith thank Him and receive a revelation of who He has made you and His character in you. You take after your Father God, you are adopted into His family. Father God sees you as His child. A child of His Kingdom, as a servant-hearted, kind steward just like Him. He has chosen you for a reason and wants to bring you into His land of promise.

God saw Moses' heart – he had seen a desire in him to save his brothers the Hebrews. On the mountain of desolation, God outlined His righteous plan and to Moses and His way to save the people. Moses encountered God in a mighty way. He got to know who God *is*; it was a type of salvation for Moses into knowing the Lord; of beginning to find his destiny as prophet and deliverer of a nation. When you know the Lord, you know more who you are and who the Lord has called you to be.

Moses felt insignificant, asking God, '*Who am I?*'. God answered Moses by saying '*certainly I shall be with you and . . . this will be a sign for you 'I AM' has sent you*' (Exodus 3:2). You may feel small and say like Moses, 'Who am I?', however the truth is that Lord God is with you and has chosen you, saved you and made you a new creation in Him. You have been chosen and called for a good reason. You are His child, part of His beloved family.

> '. . . you are the children of the city of the holy ones, with all the rights as family members of the household of God. You are rising like the perfectly fitted stones of the temple . . . your lives being built up together upon the ideal foundation laid . . . connected to the Head cornerstone . . . the Anointed One, Jesus Christ himself.'

(Ephesians 2:19-20 TPT)

When the Lord revealed His name and His holiness to Moses, He asked Moses to take off His shoes as the ground was holy. Moses obeyed the voice of the Lord. God was preparing him to be sent out. Hundreds of years later Jesus washed the disciples' feet; a faithful sign he was making them clean and holy to be sent out. Jesus has made you clean and holy to Father God through the cross; He wants you to know your Father more fully and be aligned with the destiny He has for you. Jesus commanded us to go out and share the good news of the Kingdom.

Humility is a key to approaching 'The I AM', for He is very holy. It was said of Moses he *was very humble, more than all the men'* (Numbers 12:3); he had seen God and was humbled. Humbling yourself is a key to knowing and approaching the Lord for *Holy is He.* Let us humble ourselves continually under His mighty hand.

Later in His life journey, Moses encountered the Lord *'face to face as a man speaks to his friend.'* (Exodus 33:11). Even if you do not yet know who you are in God fully, have faith by His Word that he is with you and will bring you into more fullness of identity in Him. If Moses was privileged to see Father God face to face and know Him as a friend, then how much more are you able to have access to know and experience your Father. Jesus died, rose and ascended so that you may commune with your Father God; you can continually be in His presence *now*.

This encounter with the Lord God transitioned Moses into His calling. God wants you to encounter Him, for you to be aligned with His destiny for your life; to realise more fully who you are in Him. He desires that you know and be an ambassador of His Kingdom on earth to destroy the works of the enemy.

God turned Moses' time as shepherd of sheep in the wilderness into preparation for leading the vast numbers of people out of slavery. God uses every season in your life to prepare you for that which He has called you. We are made like Him in order to set others free. Everything you have experienced is turned around for good for those who love the Lord and are called according to His purposes (Romans 8:28).

Moses saw and 'turned aside' (Exodus 3:2) to see a shrub which was burning. A burning bush would have been a usual occurrence in such hot climes. However, Moses looked carefully and realised a supernatural flame burned. I encourage you to watch carefully and 'turn aside', for your extraordinary God may be speaking to you in the ordinary of your daily life. Be aware of the Lord at all times; give your life to Him anew today. Draw near to know Him more and He will draw near to you. God is always speaking and desiring you to fully know that you are completely His! Be aware, encounter Him, seek after Him.

I turned aside from my usual activity one day when I had a specific experience of hearing God's voice which has continued to this day. In my heart I had heard Father God's voice speaking clearly, telling me that He is the 'I Am' of my life. I surrendered and began to believe Him and to trust in Him more. During this time, I was led to be involved in bringing together a planning team to mobilise thousands of followers of Jesus to go out on the streets of London to pray for healing and miracles. We were to be carriers of the command to the enemy to: 'Let My People Go!' We shared the saving grace of our Lord with many people in a predominately Muslim neighbourhood, introducing them to our loving Father and Jesus His Son.

Every day there were hundreds of testimonies of healings and miracles, and many gave their lives to Jesus. One such testimony is that a woman came with a walking stick having had a stroke and left without her stick. She went out on to the streets full of the presence of the Lord and came back giving testimony that a Muslim mother and daughter had given their lives to Jesus and were going to attend the local church. Glory to the Lord! It was such a privilege to work as Jesus' body together to bring the good news to London.

If you find yourself in a wilderness place, do not fear, it can be full of surprises, turn aside. You can trust your Father God to see your heart. Give up your own way of doing things and trust God's way through Jesus, who is The Way for your life. I pray that you will hear the voice of I AM and know that He has sent you and made you clean through His saving grace. I pray that would encounter your Lord God more deeply and be filled with His presence daily.

One example of a burning bush experience in my own life was when I witnessed beautiful waterspouts on holiday for the last few years. The Holy Spirit highlighted these occurrences to me which are linked to scripture:

Deep calls to deep at the sound of His waterspouts;
all your waves (Lord) and billows have gone over me.

(Psalm 42:8)

The Holy Spirit has encouraged me that His voice can be found in the midst of such natural wonders. God loves to call out to us and speak to us in deep and life-changing ways. God's creation is good, and he speaks through it. Keep a watch and be aware of His voice in His creation as you travel through your day.

Even in those times when it feels as though we are covered in difficulty, God's voice is right there with us speaking deeply. Listen and watch. Out of your difficulty, His Word is calling you.

Made in the likeness of I AM

Isaiah prophesied about Jesus Christ seven hundred years before the Messiah was born. The word *Christ* is the Greek translation for the Hebrew word *Messiah*.

Let us take a walk through some of Isaiah 49. These inspired words of God show us who Jesus is – and therefore who you are, because you are made in His likeness:

- It is written: *'The Lord God, who is faithful, the Holy One of Israel, who has chosen you'* (Isaiah 49:7).

  God is faithful and to be trusted, therefore so are you, because you are made like Him. You are faithful and to be trusted because He is faithful. He has faith in you, as you have faith in Him. You are made like Him, and when you give your life to Him you take on His attributes.

- It is written: *'For I AM will contend with your adversaries'* (Isaiah 49:25). I AM is the name of God Himself.

  God Himself fights for you, and you can fight for others because He first fought for you and brings you into all freedom. You are made in His likeness.

- It is written: *'And all flesh will know that I AM the Lord your deliverer and Saviour'* (Isaiah 49:26).

  God is the one who saves you, and you can save others because He first saved you. As you humble yourself under His mighty hand, Father God brings you into a place of deliverance in Jesus. You are made in His likeness.

Many times, when I hear His name, I think that yes, He is my Saviour from harm, from poverty, from hatred, and so on.

Prayer:

Thank You Father God for showing me the mystery of Your name and nature in me, and I in You.

Thank You that I dwell in Your heart, Father God; that I am Yours and that You, The I AM, are mine.

Thank you for the good plan you have for my life. Help me to listen and follow your plans and purposes.

Thank you for your Word Lord. Help me to take time to turn aside to hear and obey what you say Lord.

Thank you for making me unique in the likeness of You and that I am enabled to overflow with your goodness to others.

Show me your destined plans, your way, your truth and life.

Show me the goodness of who you are, so that I may show the same to others.

Thank you that you made me Like you Lord.

Amen.

1. http://www.abarimpublications.com/Meaning/Horeb.html#.XbLSzvZFx9A
2. https://www.youtube.com/watch?v=RJEaIGDykYE

THREE

In the Beginning, You Were Made in His Likeness

THE I AM

His shadow
Lights up your life
His arms enfold
Your small soul
His self-sacrifice
Covering
Good and ugly
Now you are
Looking more
Like the I AM

LET US THINK ABOUT THE BEGINNING. In Genesis 1, Father God, our Creator says:

> *We will make mankind in our image, after our*
> *likeness, to have dominion over the fish of the sea,*
> *over the birds of the air, over the cattle and over*
> *all the earth and every creeping thing that creeps*
> *upon the earth . . . and God blessed (you) and said:*
> *'Be fruitful and multiply!'*

(Genesis 1:26)

God desires you to know that you have 'dominion' over all things which creep! It is written that from the beginning creeping things are under your authority. Perhaps the word 'creeps' in the above text is mentioned twice to emphasise this for you.

God the Father's desire is for you to be free from all fear and deception. He means it and He is not afraid and so you need not be either. In the Gospels, Jesus told His enemy: *'It is written!'* You can therefore declare that you have freedom from fear, and that you rule over every 'creeping thing', including all the spiders and their webs and all the slithering things both natural and supernatural.

He also desires you to have dominion – to rule over all: 'all the earth'. Remember the name 'Adam' means earth and so there is a sense of ruling over death and disobedience as well as ruling over the land as an ambassador for God's Kingdom.

From the beginning, Father God made you a spiritual ruler through His authority. He gave you might, positive authority, power, and strength to rule over this earthly domain from the beginning. He is Father of all fathers and Jesus is King of all kings. You are a king made to rule and reign with Him, to see His kingdom come on earth as it is in the heavenly realms.

Being continually free from fear of the enemy is an important aspect of being Like Him. God made the serpent, our old enemy, creep on his belly, and God encourages us not to fear Satan. Time and again 'Do not be afraid' is written throughout God's Word. Father desires you to repent of any ungodly fear as it is disobedience and ask His forgiveness. You need to forgive yourself and others continually as you walk with God in love. Jesus has enabled and equipped you to rule over enemy instilled fear and to have authority over it. This authority is in the powerful, loving name of Jesus and through the strength of His Word as you meditate on it daily. You can confess His words over your life and your beloved ones and know His words in your heart: *'So if the Son sets you free from sin, then become a true son and be unquestionably free!'* (John 8:36 TPT). Let us confess our disobedience to Him and be free to receive the fullness of His freedom and the presence of His love. Let us surrender and ask the Holy Spirit to transform our minds and to fill our souls. 'Jesus died, rose and ascended for you so that you can know that you are made in the image of Father, Son and Spirit; you can receive His Father heart love for you, being made completely whole. You are being made more like Him.'

The more you are aware of Jesus' presence in you and talk and walk with Him, the more you have childlike faith and believe what *He says*. Your faith is something which grows daily as well as being a gift from God. Faith and love are the opposite of fear. Have active faith, *knowing* and receiving the love of your Father. The word 'Yada' in Hebrew is to know experientially. As you know Jesus, Father and Holy Spirit more, you will experience God's love. This love of all loves will overcome the fear in your heart and mind. In his book 'Hosting His Presence', Bill Johnson writes: *'we have been called to such intimate communication with Him that all things are possible for us who believe and who have been created like Him'.*[1]

Continually bring any fear to Him. Jesus died, rose and is seated at Fathers right hand so that you are now at liberty to walk free from the condemnation of your own thoughts and of all the enemies lies. Your spirit walked through the doorway of the cross and now resides with Him in authority in the heavenlies. I encourage you to have continual faith in God's word to remember, as it is written in Genesis, the serpent has been already cursed to 'crawl on its belly'. Realise the authority you have in Jesus and that you are made to be Like Him.

You are the beloved, breathed-into new creation of your Father God. By faith, you are freed from all roots of fear in The Name of Jesus. You are able to partner with Holy Spirit and command all roots of fear to go, generational lies to be laid low and to receive The Spirit of Truth in Jesus mighty authority. Be filled with the love and truth of God and let the seeds of His words of love grow in your mind and emotions. By faith in the name of Jesus, by the Holy Spirit and through His word, you are equipped to tear down all barriers and blockages to love. There is much more to write concerning this huge subject and we are only touching on it here as an encouragement to lean into His love for you for the freedom He has bought for you.

Praying through release from fear with spiritual experts is extremely beneficial for where two or three agree, there is freedom. I have received this kind of specific prayer when I was baptised, being cut off from my past life. For me baptism was also a key to being free from fear.

Continue to be brave and be strong in the Lord put on God's *full* armour. Put on His Salvation mindset, His strong arm of Faith, His good news gospel, the sword of His word be in your mouth, His truth around your waist daily. Cloak yourself in Him as you walk through your day. (Ephesians 6:11-18). Praying always in the Spirit, having the courage to face fear, to overcome and be an overcomer – this is your inheritance. You are a child of God, made in His image. Father God is not afraid of anything which creeps and neither need we be. Let us agree now that you will be utterly free from any fear and instead be filled with the awe of the Lord Most High. I pray that you would discover and have even more faith in your heart that you are a beloved child of your Father God, through Jesus and that you have authority over everything that creeps and crawls.

Then, by constantly using your faith, the life of Christ will be released deep inside you, and the resting place of his love will become the very source and root of your life. You will be empowered to discover what every holy one experiences – the great magnitude of the astonishing love of Christ in all its dimensions. How deeply intimate and far-reaching is his love!

> *'Endless love beyond measurement that transcends our understanding- this extravagant love pours into you until you are filled to overflowing with the fullness of God!'*

(Ephesians 3:17-19 TPT)

Whenever you face fear, ask the Holy Spirit to reveal the Father's love to you. For it is written that you have not been given a spirit of fear, but of love, power, and a sound mind.

In the beginning Father God placed Adam and Eve in a delightful garden and gave them dominion over the whole earth. He gave them and us all the freedom to choose of our own destiny or to submit to his plans through trust and obedience. We can choose whether to obey and submit to His ways and instructions or whether not to. Adam and Eve decided to disobey God after He gave them just one rule. Instead they listened to the Satan's deception (*Satan* is the Hebrew word for 'enemy'). Their obedience was tested and found wanting. They surrendered their authority over all the earth to the father of all lies. Satan is the god of this world, and he rules the earth and the worldly systems. Before Jesus was tempted in the wilderness, and after the enemy showed Him all the wealth of the earth, he said to Jesus:

I shall give you authority over all this, and their glory, because it has been given over to me and I could give it to whomever I wish.

(Luke 4:6)

Satan had fallen from Heaven and ruled over the earth until Jesus came to save us from Satan's dominion. The enemy's rule is primarily through strategic deception, possession of souls, and manipulation of mankind. We overcome the rule of Satan as we become transformed into the likeness of our true Lord Jesus and Father God, and as we learn to live, dwell and become more Like Him. We enforce the victory of the cross on earth as it is in heaven.

Father God's amazing plan to overcome the enemy's rule on earth was to send the last 'Adam' (1 Corinthians 15:45-49) who is Jesus, our salvation. Through His death and resurrection, Jesus been given authority over all the earth and when you receive Him, He dwells within you by His Spirit! The cross of Jesus is a doorway into the kingdom of the heavenly realms. When you seek after God's will as you journey through life, you enable the righteous kingdom of the heavenlies to be manifested on the earth. As you move into who God is and who you really are, you become full of the loving authority of God. All glory to Him because of who He is and what He has done in you already.

There has been a spiritual battle happening ever since a third of heaven fell to earth, and since the deception and disobedience of mankind. This battle is fought in the mind, in the physical body, and in the spiritual world. Our fellow Christian leader Paul writes and encourages us in this battle, saying that once we have committed our lives to Father God and Jesus, we can 'put on' our new selves. We are continually being renewed in regard to our behaviour and mindset, into the likeness of our Creator.

The following verse implies that this is an active faith-renewal walk, not a passive reception:

> *You must not lie to one another since you are stripped off of the old person with his or her deeds, and by putting on your new self, which is being renewed in knowledge according to the image of the One who created the universe.*

(Colossians 3:9)

It is written in Colossians 2:15 that by dying on the cross, Jesus *'disarmed the principalities and authorities, when He triumphed over them'*. Also, in Revelation, the Messiah Jesus speaks: *I am living forever, and I have the keys of death and Hades'*. Our Messiah has been given 'All authority . . . in heaven and on earth' and He has given us permission to go out in His name to destroy the works of Satan on earth.

In Ephesians, Paul writes this about what God did for His Son:

> *'. . . He seated Him on His right hand in the heavenlies far above every rule and authority and power and dominion . . . . He made all things subject under His feet and gave Him authority over everyone in the congregation.'*

(Ephesians 1:20-23)

The apostles wrote that you have the likeness of Jesus when you give your life continually to Him, because those who love God *'have the same form of the likeness of His Son'* (Romans 8:29).

Father God made you like Himself and He accepts you. You are qualified through cross of Jesus. His Kingdom accepts those who are weak because your life is strong when it is dependent on His strength and not your own. He knows that you are on a journey of being transformed into His likeness. You rule and reign in and through Him and can, through His authority, enforce His victory on earth, as it is in His heavenly Kingdom.

Father God accepts you, and longs to have a close, intimate relationship with you. The Father and Son paid a huge price so that you can know them intimately. Let us decide to be defined by how our Father accepts us, rather than be defined by how other people look at you. You are a new creation, accepted and favoured because He has chosen you. It is written: *'He favoured us with the Beloved One',* and, *'He made us accepted in the Beloved'* (Ephesians 1:6 NKJV). You are made in His likeness.

I myself have often felt misunderstood by people in the past, mainly perhaps due to lack of communication on my part or theirs. However, I know God knows my heart and He knows your heart on every matter. I have learnt not to be offended by others disjointed views as they do not know my heart like our Father God does. We can forgive as we have been forgiven. You are a new creation by His grace, and you are known by your Father God. It is written: *'How thoroughly you know me, Lord!'* (Psalm 139:14 TPT)

Be defined by the likeness of who you really are in God, and what His word says about you not by what others say or perceive you to be. It says in His word *'Your understanding of me brings me wonder and strength'* (Psalm 139:6 TPT) You are made in the likeness of the Most High God, who is good; who is right and kind. When you turn from everything that is not of His will, He forgives. Ask Him to show you more of the truth about who you are.

Your Father God sees you as your perfect, righteous, heavenly self. Thank the Father that you are forgiven by the blood love of Jesus, so that you can forgive others. You can decide not to be defined by your own feelings or perception about yourself; but be defined instead by what He says about you. You can meditate on the fact that: *'He keeps my feet from stumbling'* (Jude 1:24) and that, I am: *'fearfully and wonderfully made'* (psalm 139). You can turn and repent from any wrong perception of yourself and any negative internal or external self-talk. Ask God to help you see yourself how He sees you and speak about yourself according to His words.

You are safe to fully surrender your heart of hearts to Him. All that is loving, all that is righteously Him is yours. When you do so, His desires become yours and your desires are His. He sees your spirit and your heart. He sees you transformed into the likeness of Jesus when you surrender your spirit, body and mind to His Spirit and His Word. Focus on His Spirit and meditate in His Word – magnify Him in your heart. Righteousness and Peace will begin to take over your body, mind and emotions.

Every day you can present yourself perfect to Father God through the blood of our sacrificial Messiah Jesus. We are weak but He is strong. He has done it, He has paid for you to be righteous before Father God, healed and whole! It is finished!

Prayer:

Lord, I surrender my all to you. My desire is for You Lord, to delight in Your ways, will and desires. May I know You more Lord God, may I know the deepness of Your love for me.

Thank You for accepting me just as I am. I am Yours. I trust You Lord. Show me and remind me by Your Word, of the truth of who I am *in* You.

Thank You, Lord for breaking the walls of fear and deception down in my mind and emotions. I praise You that I am free because of Your word and Your great truth and love for me.

Thank You for continually forgiving me of all ungodly fear, guilt and shame and releasing me from all their affects. I declare that ungodly fear no longer belongs to me.

I receive Your abundant love in the place of the fear that was there. Thank You for loving me so extravagantly Lord.

Thank You for forgiving me of all negative self-talk and perception which are not from You. Help me to be aware of this and for my mind to be transformed to be like Yours.

I forgive myself and declare that I am no longer condemned. I am made to be like You, Lord God, one who rules and reigns *in* You. Your ambassador in the earth. Thank you for everything You have given me, I am equipped with everything I need.

Thank You that I am a new creation, I am being transformed into Your likeness more every day.

Amen.

---

1. Hosting the Presence, Bill Johnson, 2013, Destiny Image

FOUR

When we see Him, we become Like Him

Breath
Making life and light
Being called
Out of darkness
A new day begins
And you are re-created
In resemblance of your Creator
In looks
In feeling
In love

THE FIRST FOLLOWERS watched our Saviour Jesus die on a cross and thereafter saw Him in His risen bodily form many times in different places. He was talking, eating, and performing wonders just as He had told them would happen. For forty days this occurred, and since then many more followers have seen Him in various different ways – bodily, in visions, in dreams, or in perception.

Christophany, or seeing Jesus, is becoming more and more common. Having fellowship with Jesus in this way for some is a part of the process of being transformed to be more like Him. Those we spend time with we become more like. Would you like to see Jesus? You can ask God to reveal

Himself, to see Jesus and know Him more; thereafter you will be transformed more into His likeness, which pleases your Father in heaven.

Throughout the second half of 2018, I had a recurring vision of Jesus as the 'Light of the world'. In the vision, there is a dark in the background and He is walking out away from this black stark, darkness. He walked in flowing white robes, which were radiant with light. The light emanating from Him is super-bright white and fascinating. He walked as a King with authority and flair, and He and His clothes were moving in a flowing way. His garments cascaded with light, and He walked toward us as light for this dark world, and as both King and Judge.

In His hand He had a book and I had been wondering what the book signified. During a meeting in worship I saw this vision once more and this time Jesus handed the book to me. It looked like a typical student file and on the front it read: 'Your Life'.

I looked inside and read the title on the first page of lined paper: it read 'Treetops'. As I was looking at the page and 'went into' the actual page (the page transitioned me to a place). I found myself with Jesus in a tree house at the top of a tree in a big forest. We were very high up and the forest was a jungle type with a vast number of trees in all directions. We could see over the treetops and as we were doing so, I saw some smoke a little way to the right of us. I knew this was produced by a large fire below and that it was a righteous fire and not to be afraid. It was similar to the fire at the burning bush experience; the fire did not burn the trees.

I turned to see Jesus' reaction and as I did, he motioned to follow him down. We descended from the tall tree to the woods below. We moved to where the fire was and were engulfed in Holy flames.

We then ascended another treehouse which was inside this fire. When we got to the top there were lots of people. They were fiery lovers of the Lord, this contrasted with the earlier tree house, where it was just me and Jesus. We joined these fiery ones in the tree-top fire house of the Lord himself.

I believe the interpretation is simply to follow the Lord, to press into His presence and go up higher together. Let us be seeking and following Jesus, enjoying His fiery presence and the journey as we ascend with Him.

'My presence will go with you, and I shall give you rest'

(Exodus 33:14)

On the first day of creation, God divided the light from the darkness, or as a teacher once told me: 'He drew the light out of the darkness'. He said: *'it was good'*.

God is always looking for the brightness or the shining 'gold' in his creation. Let us have compassion just as God has compassion on the people we meet and see 'the gold' in them. They may then see the true Light of Life on and in us. Have faith and show the love of the Lord God so that they will desire to seek The Light of the World, our Lord of Righteousness, Jesus!

This happened when I first met my friend Angie. I felt God's huge compassion for her and poured out His words for her. This enabled her to receive Jesus into her life anew. Angie has testified that she saw a light shining over me, which was His glory. She is following Jesus to this day. We are most like Him when we give of ourselves, for He is a giving God.

Let us share the light.

Prayer:

Thank You, Father God, for Your Son's empathy, for the lens of Your love, for the ability to see the gold even in the darkness of people's lives.

I receive the enablement of the Holy Spirit to see people like the Father sees them.

I want to take Your love and your light wherever I go, thank you Lord.

Amen.

Name Above All

The Hebrew name for Jesus is Yeshua, which means 'saviour, deliverer'. Think about swapping the word 'Saviour' or 'Deliverer' for the name Jesus at times, when you read the Bible. Likewise, when you read the word 'saved', 'salvation' or 'saves', you can read it as 'Jesus'. For instance, *'He only is my Rock and my Salvation'* would read: *'He only is my Rock and my Jesus'.* (psalm 62:3). Jesus' name is revealed in this way throughout the old testament. This has given me more depth of revelation of His Word as I read, I trust it will for you.

There are other interesting revelations concerning Jesus' name. For instance, Jesus was asked who He was several times in the Gospel of John. One of these powerful moments was in the garden of Gethsemane, when a centurion asked which one of the crowd He was before His arrest, Jesus answered *'I AM'* and *'the entire arresting party, fell to the ground.'* (John 18:6).

As alluded to before, these two words in Hebrew have significant meaning as they are the name of God Himself. It seems here that when Jesus uttered The Name of who He is, was and will be, the power knocked a crowd of soldiers to the ground! A similar manifestation happens at times when people fall down under the power of His name. I pray you remember the revelation of His name and its importance as you read the Bible. When we are transformed more into His likeness by surrendering our own self, and when we live His presence, each of us can also say 'I am like the I AM'.

In the beginning, Father God gave Adam the duty of naming all the animals. This is a wonderful and powerful responsibility God has given each of us; to name children, places, animals and things. Our parents named each of us with a special name and I have found that discovering the meaning of that name is very helpful in knowing that which God has destined for us. It may not be the whole picture of my destiny on earth, but my name offers insight into a role I am called to, or an aspect of how that role will come about. For instance, my first name is Julia, which means 'youthful', and God has given me a childlike heart and faith, which helps me have a deeper relationship with Him (*unless you would change and become like the children, you will be no means enter the Kingdom of the Heavens*' Matthew 18:3).

This has grown as I have realised that I am youthful forever in Him and can sit on Father's lap of love and whisper to Him. I have found that my prayers are always answered as we spend time together.

I encourage you to find out the meaning behind your names from a Hebraic perspective, while at the same time asking Father God how this may link up with who you are and with His destiny for you on earth. Perhaps this will be of help to you on your journey of life. I pray it will be so.

One example of the power of names was found when I ministered in the shopping mall as a street pastor. I used to ask people their names and read them a name meaning and give a scripture to go with it. A few times Holy Spirit gave me a word of knowledge about the person's current employment due to their name meaning. I used *The Name Book* by Dorothy Astoria[1] which gives insight into the meaning, along with a scripture. This enabled me to have a more confident prophetic flow from Holy Spirit for them.

For instance, I remember telling a woman named Susan that her name means 'purity'. I asked if she happened to be a nurse and her answer was yes. I had learnt from Holy Spirit that the name Susan may indicate a more caring strength of personality and I believe this enabled a word of knowledge from God in this particular instance. This helped Susan to know that God is real and He was interested in her life. I was able to share with her about Jesus her Saviour more easily thereafter. This outflowing of words of knowledge enables others to have more faith that God is speaking to them directly, and that He loves them.

A study into the original meaning of words in scripture often aids the reader into a living and more deeply revelatory experience. Each word in the original Hebrew of the older testament of the Bible has deep levels of meaning which also link to the newer testament. For instance, the God of Abraham, Isaac, and Jacob is the God of *Israel*. One meaning of the name Israel is 'to struggle or wrestle with God and man'[2]; another meaning is 'a prince or princess of God'.

As you read God's living Word, keep in mind the meaning behind this name Israel. As you read the living words of God, knowing the fuller meaning will help you better identify with the Spirit of the Lord in Scripture:

> Let **Israel** hope in the LORD, for with the LORD
> there is loving-kindness, and plenteous redemption
> is with Him.

> (Psalm 130:7)

As well as considering the word Israel as identifying the nation, you can also apply this to yourself and read it as *'Let the one who struggles with God hope in the Lord'*. Another example is the name 'Noah' which means 'comfort' in Hebrew. The Lord God comforted the whole of creation through this great man, who had faith and obeyed Father God by building The Ark (or 'box') causing mankind to continue to multiply by taking his sons and their wives with him. The Lord God comforted us all through Noah/Comfort by making a promise to never again destroy the earth by flooding. The Lord sent and is still sending us His rainbow sign of comfort to remind us all of His mercy towards us.

Discovering the meaning of names of prominent people and places in the Bible is a great blessing which uncovers many treasures. For example, Moses, whose name means 'one drawn out of water' and who aptly led the nation of Israel out of the waters of the Red Sea and into the wilderness. Moses led them out of Egypt (meaning 'narrow place') into the vastness of the wilderness or 'place of speaking'.

Just like the meaning of 'Israel', you may at times have struggled with the Lord God Himself. It stands to reason that if you struggle with who God is, you may also struggle with knowing who you are at times, since you are made in His likeness. Although you struggle, you can still hope and have faith in this struggle. There is a time to let go and trust God.

Like Jacob did when he was struggling with the angel of the Lord, you can let go and trust that God is on your side and that He is working out all things for your good (Jeremiah 29) even though it may not seem that way in the natural, faith believes that which it cannot see (Hebrews 11:1). When you let go and have faith you become Israel: 'a prince/princess of The Lord' who has faith that God is good all the time. You are made in God's very likeness, you resemble Him.

There are many places in Scripture where the meaning of the name 'Israel' is 'prince of God'. I have inserted the deeper meaning of the name as follows: 'Let me, the prince [or princess] in the Lord, hope in the Lord'.

Which person are you? A prince/princess of God or one who struggles with Him? Perhaps we are (or have been) both, depending on our place in the journey of life.

When you know who God is more fully, then you will see your true self, because you will understand things from His perspective; the way He sees you. This is the true you. You are a prince or princess in God's kingdom.

The struggles in your past can bring you to the place of surrender to Jesus, who died and suffered so that you might move into a place of freedom. The more you know Father, Jesus, and Holy Spirit, the more your true identity comes into focus. Then you see and know who you are in the I AM.

You can trust in God and His good character. He is often drawing you close. Much of your struggle can be solved by letting go to trust Him completely in a childlike fashion. God also trusts *you*, in that He entrusted you with His entire creation and the rulership of it. How trusting He is! For you, He sent His Son to live, suffer, die, and be resurrected. You can trust Him due to His vast sacrificial love. You are very valuable to Him.

Father God says this to you: *'I have loved you with an everlasting love. Therefore, I have drawn you with loving-kindness'* (Jeremiah 31:3 NKJV).

Prayer:

Thank You Lord, that You know my name.

Let me know what this means for my life.

Thank You, that You are my powerful Saviour, Jesus.

Thank You for the deep meaning You bring to my life.

I trust in You. Please forgive me where I have not trusted in You.

I am in awe of You and choose not to lay any blame in Your camp.

Thank You for forgiving me and fighting for me.

I humble myself under Your capable hands.

I trust You to lead shape my life.

Thank You that I am grafted into Your kingdom, I am a prince/ess in Your eyes.

May I be more like You, may I know who I am in You more.

Amen.

---

1. The Name Book, Dorothy Astoria, Bethany House, 2008
2. Genesis 32:29 'Your name will no longer be called Jacob, but Israel, for as a prince you have power with God and with men and you have prevailed'. (ONMB – the note in this translation sheds even deeper meaning on Jacob and Israel's two names: one of Jacob meanings is to 'Follow Close after, to heed (God's will) and another meaning of Israel is: 'prevailing with God'.

FIVE

Ruling and Reigning in His Love

Give up the rule of your own self-kingship
Spirit, body, and soul
Give up to the King of all
Who knows you fully
Give up, to sit down
Beside Him in peace
Give up to rule with Him
In His kingdom of glory

Our High Priest and King has shown us His sacrificial love so that now we are able to trust Him implicitly, unlike others before Him. We can talk with Him on an intimate level and yet He is also to be honoured and reverenced due to the loftiness of who He is.

There is one aspect of His Priesthood which may help us; a higher level of priestly identity we can know in Him. It is written that Jesus is operating within the priestly order of Melchizedek (Hebrews 6:20). 'Melech' means 'King' in Hebrew and Zedek means 'righteous priest'. The whole meaning is: 'King of peace and righteousness/justice'. Jesus is our High Priest and King in this order and not in the Levitical Order.

I believe we are priests and kings according to the order of Melchizedek, as we operate in kingdom authority to rule and reign through Jesus, who is of the same order (see Hebrews 7). This is our princely endorsement from the Most High. This is a glorious calling for the princes and princesses of the Most High God. As you humble yourself you are elevated with Him. Let us remain humble in Him and trust Our King, who always does the right thing to bring us peace and justice.

As a son or daughter of Father God, you serve as a prince becoming a king and priest in the likeness of the resurrected Jesus, who is your High Priest.

Psalms says that when we *'sit enthroned under the shadow of Shaddai'*, then we are *'hidden in the strength of God Most High'* (Psalm 91:1 TPT). This shows that we have a throne near to God Himself, our provider and maker. We can be 'enthroned' in Him. When you choose to sit down and be enthroned in the rest of God Himself, you can be sure of His strength for your life. Your full inheritance of being a king or queen is to be seated on a throne to rule and reign with Jesus, your Bridegroom King.

After Jesus rose again, He went to sit at the right hand of God the Father. When we are *in Him*, we are spiritually in the same place as He is. In the eastern ancient world, the kings and queens sat down to judge and give rulings, judgments and declarations. Sitting on their throne indicated their authority, while the courtiers before them stood up. For instance, in gatherings, those with the authority would be the only ones seated. In the western world, this rule is often reversed, with the most important person standing while the rest of the gathering is seated.

There is a 'throne' inside of you. A place of spiritual rest, you can be 'sat down' in the spirit and in the heavenlies. Sit down, and lean into His rest in your heart, mind, and body. You can rule with your Messiah in this spiritual place of contentment; a place of abundance; a place where your Saviour King resides within you. Let Him continually rule the throne of your spirit on earth as in heaven. Take a deep breath in right now and receive His restful presence. Breathe out all that is not of Him. Rest in Him.

Together, He and you can be spiritually ruling in authority from the heavenlies above, declaring good and loving things and affecting the atmosphere and reality of the earth beneath. He is ascended and calls us to share His victory with Him. We can agree with the battle plans of Father, Son and Spirit and see what the Father is doing, just like Jesus did when on earth.

We can pray from this place and enable heaven to break through into earth's realm.

> *'And I will give you the keys of the kingdom of heaven and whatever you bind on Earth will be bound in heaven, and whatever you loose on Earth will be loosed in heaven.'*

> (Matthew 16:19 NKJV)

We can rest in the knowledge that our prayers are heard by our Father God when we learn to live from this place as we spiritually reside close to Him.

I have had multiple visions of the throne of grace which the Father has given me. When I am interceding, I can often see the place of rulership and rest from which I pray – from heaven to earth in the authority of Jesus Himself, who is ruling in me on earth as High Priest, and beside me in the heavens as King of all kings.

Father God has given me confidence and more faith to know that my prayers are heard and I now trust Him to answer them in His way. God is a compassionate Father who will listen to those who have a close relationship with Him and intercede on behalf of others.

Our Father is moved by our prayers, Moses prayed and interceded on behalf of a whole nation and moved the Lord's heart towards the people of Israel.

Perhaps God's throne moves when His sons and daughters mercifully pray? He has chosen a moveable throne, with wheels; it is a chariot throne (Daniel 7:9). Our Father's character never changes, and He is holy. At the same time, He has chosen to be merciful and listen to our entreaties and is moved when our hearts are merciful just like His heart.

You have a throne in heaven such as the one I have seen. Ask for eyes to see and knowledge to know that you are seated with Father and Jesus in heavenly realms.

This seat and relationship with Father God, is the connection and authority that Adam had with Him in the garden of Eden, before mankind's disobedience occurred. This is the place of relationship which Jesus restored at the cross. Father resurrected Jesus to rule His heavenly kingdom, and eventually He will restore all things through His kingdom rule and reign. In the meantime, through Jesus, you are able to live and rest in the delight and favour of God Himself. Jesus is a servant King, the King of all kings, your perfect example of a king, and you are a king or queen in and of His kingdom. You are true royalty.

> 'A righteous ruler sits on his or her throne of right justice. . . . He or she scatters evil away' from their domain of influence and authority.
>
> (Proverbs 20:8 Paraphrased)

> 'Lovers of God have been given eyes to see with spiritual discernment and ears to hear what Father God is speaking.'
>
> (Proverbs 20:12 TPT)

One of the key words is *discernment* in the scripture above. By the Spirit of God, you can receive discernment continually. Right now, you can receive Father's discernment and wisdom from above on how to judge or assess the situation before you. You can judge from this place of holy, higher discernment. This is a place not made by us but given freely to you by Him, through the Beloved One (He is the one who gives us access). How wonderful, kind and trusting is our God and King! He is a truly giving and trusting Father who allows you to rule and reign with Him. Ask for access to hear, see, and understand what He wants to give you, where He wants you to rule and reign, and what His plans are for you.

Jesus presently resides in the heavenly realms at the right hand of the Father. You can walk through life in faith that your saving King says, '*All authority has been given to Me in heaven and upon the earth*' (Matthew 28). This echoes the words written in Genesis, when Father God gave Adam and Eve authority over all the earth. Now Jesus has been given all authority over heaven and earth and He is in you and as you surrender, His authority flows through you.

As you live with and have faith in the resurrection and ascension of your Immanuel, you can call upon and rest in His authority, to rule and reign with Him.

When He lived on earth before dying and rising from the dead, Jesus ruled over elements of the earth. Let us consider the role He modelled. For example, consider what Ian Johnson points out in *What Is Mankind* :[1]

- Yeshua governed over substance when He changed water into wine (John 2:1-11).

- Yeshua ruled over the elements when He calmed the storm (Mark 4:35-41).

- Yeshua ruled over enemy beings when He cast out demonic entities (Mark 9:17-27).

- Yeshua ruled over sickness when He healed people numerous times (Matthew 15:29-31).

- Yeshua governed His human body when He disappeared before their eyes (John 8:56-59; Luke 4:28-30).

- He ruled over time when the boat He was in was transported suddenly and miraculously to the shore (John 6:16).

I believe this divine authority is yours as you submit to His Way, Truth and Life and become 'one' with Him (John 17). He also spoke and told us that we would do *greater works* (John 14:12) which many of us are longing to be a part of. Jesus is ascended now and as you continually commune with Him, and in Him, may these greater works flow through you.

The Hebrew meaning of *Immanuel* is 'God with us'. In Him we have loving authority 'over all the earth' because of our relationship with and in Him.

> *'He made us alive in Messiah ... and He raised us together and caused us to sit down together in the heavenlies with Messiah Yeshua'*
>
> (Ephesians 2:5-6)

I have been given a simple song to sing by Holy Spirit which recurs inside my heart often which helps me be more aware of Him in me. It goes like this:

There is a place where love does dwell.
There is a name: Immanuel
He dwells inside,
He dwells within,
In unseen realm so real, so true.
The King of all, He dwells in you.

Each day, you can live and move and have your being continually in Him so that you are able to move in His righteous authority which transforms not only you but everything around you. You can access the kingdom of the heavenlies and do not have to wait to enter into the promised eternal life. You can live and move and have your being now in Him, *who is your righteousness*. Of course, there is still more fulfilment to come in terms of being wholly in His heavenly kingdom, when you leave this earth and your body dies, you will live in His Kingdom presence together in unity fully. However, there is still much more to discover here on earth about who you are in God, so that you become more like Him in order to do His will on earth as it is in the heavenlies.

As you rest in the presence of Jesus, Father, and Holy Spirit on the throne in your heart, you can declare righteousness and justice from this place; that the Father's will is done.

You have received so much good from God in your spirit, mind, and body, and now you are able to powerfully impact for good, everyone around you. When we hear and speak out His will on earth, it moves the thrones in heaven to release justice, peace, and joy.

Our Father in heaven has chosen us to enforce the work of the cross on the earth. The powerful kingdom and will of Father God is continually done on the earth as it is in heaven as we become ever more like Him; believe, declare and take action.

Let us declare our righteous King's Kingdom come:

> We declare the blood of Jesus over ourselves and our family today!
>
> We declare the peace of God over our loved ones today!
>
> We declare righteousness and justice over all our situations today!
>
> We declare the love and protection of God over loved ones and ourselves today!
>
> We declare the healing power of God over our family today!
>
> We declare peace and joy over our ourselves and our colleagues in business today!
>
> We declare the victory of righteousness and justice over our whole household today!
>
> We declare the victory of righteousness and justice over our town today!
>
> We thank you Lord that we can rest in your peace in all we do this day.

Let us again surrender all our earthly battles to Him and lean into Him. You can give all earthly needs and desires to Him and delight yourself in Him, for He really does care for you! Then rule and reign with Him in His resurrection power.

> *'For you died and your life has been hidden with the Messiah in God'.*

> (Colossians 3:3)

*'Then if you died with Messiah, we are believing
that we will also live with Him.'*

(Romans 6:8)

Finally, I would like to share a vision with you which I received
with regards moving with Jesus in the storms. I was walking
in heaven with Jesus on a surface which was very light blue in
colour. There were gently undulating waves. These waves
were minimal and uniform, not at all like the more random
waves of earth, which are whipped up by the wind. Jesus and
I were holding hands and as I watched a song sprang up from
my heart:

Let us walk hand in hand
Step across this heavenly land
I will guide you step by step
You can walk on water

After a while, I found myself on earth in the biblical scene
in which Jesus walks on the water in a storm. I could see the
disciples' boat, and Jesus and Peter were walking on water.
I watched Peter move toward the Lord, and then the scene
paused as if on a video screen. It was like a snapshot vision
which I saw after this, and although I kept watching and I
hoped for the vision to carry on and move forward, it was
fixed with Peter walking successfully on the moving waves
with hands reaching out to Jesus. The waves were rough and
quite steep, especially compared to the previous heavenly
gentle undulation.

I watched and rested in the paused vision and I asked Jesus:
'Is there something I needed to learn from this?' I waited
patiently and He showed me that it was ironical that Peter,
whose name means 'rock', was the disciple to walk on water

with Him, since his name denoted that he was the one most likely to sink! Jesus said, 'If Peter, my beloved disciple can walk on water, so can you!' Jesus showed me that He has done everything in the atonement so that we are able to do the wonders He has already done.

I had a sense that the walking on water was primarily indicative of aspects in our lives that are seemingly impossible, where we seem surrounded by stormy difficulties. He was showing me that we can overcome by easily walking spiritually over the difficulty by walking hand in hand with Him, and that we can be supernaturally balanced by faith in Him.

Jesus emphasised the stormy waves to me; that He walked on waves which were rocking up and down. Not only did Jesus defeat the laws of physics, He also has tremendous balancing skills! The Hebrew word that means 'balance' denotes honesty and truth at its root. He was showing me that this is a key to overcoming. Always be honestly wise with God and with man about your situation and watch what happens.

He reminded me that when He walked on water, He had not yet died, risen or ascended. How much more am I able to overcome now Jesus has died, risen and is seated at the Father's right hand! Due to my relationship with the Messiah, I am enabled to 'walk on the water' and overcome difficulties, fears, anxiety, or whatever I face. I can cast all my care upon Him and I can focus on Him. I can 'walk' with Him through life, spiritually speaking, from a more elevated, gentle place inside myself; seeing the bigger picture, when I hold on to Him and focus on Him. My soul can rest and walk the undulating and peaceful waves.

Let us ask Jesus, our Messiah, for supernatural, honest balance in our lives, and for ability to overcome by walking hand in hand with Him as the world rocks around us. When we focus on Him, we will not sink like a rock into an emotional or circumstantial turbulence, but will stand and walk with Him, our Rock of salvation. Let us walk with Him on the undulating peaceful waves in the heavenlies.

Prayer:

We desire to seek after Your face, Father; we want to wait on You, and to hear and see that which You are doing in heaven and on earth.

We worship You in Spirit and truth, and desire to be a sweet fragrance to You.

Lord we want to walk with You in Your Peace. We receive Your Shalom right now. Thank You for being the rock of our salvation.

Thank You for enabling us to enter Your rest and to be overcomers.

We thank You, Father, that You are pleased when we work together with You to rule and reign as Your sons and daughters of Your kingdom.

Thank you that we are seated with you Jesus in the heavenlies and that You bring about Your righteousness and justice upon the earth as it is in heaven where there is no pain, calamity or evil works.

Help us use Your/our God-given authority to destroy the works of the evil one where we are right now.

Praise You Lord!

Amen

---

1. What is Mankind, Ian Johnson, His Amazing Glory Media, 2019

SIX

Sanctuary

I am a tent
I am a temple
I am a habitation
I am who You say I am
'Made in heaven' is on my tag
Inside you'll find
A box of the Word alive
A table of bread so fresh
A lamp with oil lit
Oil from olives crushed
Supply from the Spirit
Life, Truth, and Way

I BELIEVE THAT THE UNDERSTANDING behind our being a temple of the Holy Spirit can help you know who you are in more depth.

In the kingdom of heavenlies there is a temple; *'For He has looked down from the height of his sanctuary.'* (Psalm 102:19). Father God asked Moses' to create a reflection of this heavenly temple on the earth in the form of a tabernacle, where God the Father could meet with mankind. When Jesus came to earth, He spent many hours in the temple in Jerusalem, meeting with the people and priests. Here was the Son of God, Jesus, God Himself, meeting mankind again in the temple, face to face.

In the Bible, Jesus told the priests that the temple, or sanctuary, which is a word nearer to original Hebrew, *'will be torn down and rebuilt in three days'* (John 2:18). Jesus was referring to His own physical, mental, spiritual existence on earth.

As Paul writes,

> *Do you not know that your body is a sanctuary of the Holy Spirit in you, which you have from God, and you do not belong to yourselves?*

> (1 Corinthians 6:19)

These verses indicate that our bodies are designed as a holy sanctuary built by God; the representation of Father God's sanctuary on earth.

Moses tabernacle was movable, and it reflected the nomadic life of the nation and perhaps the beginnings of humankind's spiritual wandering. It can also be symbolic of your own journey as a 'Christ-one'. Our lives may be in a place of wandering, not fully rooted, and yet established in our faith. Our spiritual life may be nomadic, as we move from one wilderness, or 'speaking place' to another.

In contrast, the second and third 'sanctuaries' were built of stone. They were permanently placed on a rock foundation and a high place in Jerusalem, meaning city of Peace. (1 Kings 8). The temple is symbolic of a more mature spiritual standing:

> *Until we would attain in the unity of faith and the knowledge of the Son of God, into a mature person, to the measure of the full maturity of the Messiah . . . that being truthful in love we would bring to*

> *maturity all the things in Him . . . . He is making*
> *the body grow, building itself up in love.*
>
> (Ephesians 4:13)

The Bible shows us a picture of the progressively better places of worship designed by God, which point to the ongoing upward process of God's relationship, or meeting place with mankind both individually and corporately. The sanctuary in spiritual terms, is an image of our mature relationship with God in the priestly sense; a pattern of how much we look in the likeness of Jesus.

Your body is like the temple building; the inner courts being the holy place of communion with God himself. As you may have heard, the curtain of the earthly temple was torn in two when Jesus died enabling us to approach 'the most holy place' to talk to your Father God. By the Spirit, Jesus our High Priest, resides inside your inner person. Through His Holy Spirit, He enables you to be continually lit with His Holy light.

We are a new spiritual temple for Him to inhabit when we are saved. The new covenant Jesus has made for us through the cross means we are able to receive His new creative life in our beings. We are a sanctuary for Him to inhabit, to bring Him glory.

This new sanctuary is still on earth and so needs to be maintained. A clean sanctuary is one which is mature, where the Spirit of the Lord desires to dwell continually, for He is Holy. Out of our love for the Lord let us seek His righteousness steadfastly. Let us desire to *'be Holy because I AM Holy'* (1 Peter 1:16). His Word encourages us to be Holy nearly twenty times throughout the new and older testaments, so this is important to Father God.

One of God's names, which indicates His character is 'YHVH Makkedesh – The Lord God who sanctifies you' or who makes you holy. His character and grace enable you to love Him and desire to know Him more; to keep His instructions and His commands in the Bible. It is written that there is a blessing in keeping His instructions. If being Holy is part of who He is, then you are made to be Like Him.

He gave you His Word so that you would know Him more and *the Way* He likes to do things. If you love Him, you will desire to obey Him. The more you know Him, His Word and His love, the less disobedient you want to be and therefore become more like Him.

By His Word and Holy Spirit, you are made holy, becoming more akin to Him. We are to be set apart for God, which is what holiness means. Mistakes, disobedience and ungodly behaviour, cause uncleanliness within us and I believe these can open the door to enemy spiritual influence.

Do you want a sanctuary body and soul full of His Spirit? We all face choices of obedience or disobedience to God's righteous way every day. Let us seek after His righteous way of doing things, of saying things and going about our day. Let us not live by our own way of doing things. Let us walk with Him in grace. If we slip up unintentionally, we can ask forgiveness for this lack. Father loves you to walk in forgiveness and to forgive others continually, so that the sanctuary of your life has no weeds of bitterness within it.

When you are born again you are a new creation and all things are new, sparkling clean. At the same time there is a need to go and 'sin no more', like Jesus said to the woman caught in adultery and the man whose eyes were miraculously opened in John's gospel. God helps us in our daily life when we ask Him not to be led into temptation or into evil; we can pray continually.

Let us be in constant communication with our Lord in many ways, sending up a sweet aroma of prayer throughout our day. Prayer and speaking in our heavenly language are so important in our lives as believers. As is supporting each other in prayer, friendship and fellowship; to keep the sanctuaries of our bodies and souls clean so that we can be filled to overflowing with spiritual light, with His word and goodness.

His holiness abides within your spirit already. Your body and soul are supernaturally enabled to love, to be peaceful and joy filled. The sanctuary of your body and soul is continually pleasing to the Lord when His holiness is maintained inside and outside of yourself. His glorious light and fire can then fill you up and this is where heaven meets earth. The overflow of His presence within you causes wonderful things to happen.

You may be wondering if this spiritual life is all about maintenance and *working out your salvation*. I think of life as a journey to the throne of Father God. There is the finished work of the cross which we can have faith to receive; this is always available until Jesus returns. We have entered the King's domain, the very Kingdom of the Lord Most High. We do not have need to go back through the cross again as this work is already done in our lives. However, we can show others how to receive and know Jesus by going to the cross. We also travel through a baptism of water and then spiritual fire on our way to the awesome throne of Father God and Jesus our Messiah. During our life journey, remembering that which God has done for us is paramount. Jesus was a carpenter, when on earth, and I have heard it said by Dr Bradford et al, that the word used in the Bible for 'carpenter', is more akin to 'builder' or even a master builder[1].

There is a sense that with our builder, Jesus, together we maintain our temple life, as we commune with Him. This makes the 'maintenance' of our lives a collaborative effort with His grace, wisdom, understanding, and so on. Our compliance to His word, our agreement, our ideas through partnership with Him, develop who we really are; so that we can show others who God really is.

We are made in His image and our communion with Him is of great importance to staying healed, whole and stable as a person, in order to model and be ambassadors of His Kingdom on earth. God is perfect and holy; we shall be wholly perfect like Him when we are fully in His Kingdom. In the meantime, let us maintain our relationship and be different than the world by focusing on our perfect Lord and desire to behave like Him.

Our relationship with Father in heaven needs looking after. Our Father is set apart from the world. He is Holy and we are made in His likeness. We are to be set apart, or a *'peculiar people'* is how the scripture puts it. We are to be separated from evil and separated for God's purpose. The role-model of Jesus and His disciples, who walked with the Father is to be a focus. They were all of Jewish descent, hence their history, language and cultural context are helpful in understanding Father God's viewpoint more clearly, so that we can be a delight to Him and be set apart from the world.

One of the main commands of the Father was to rest every week on the sabbath. Rest is a focus of the Father. One fine day our journey will end with our spirit being completely at rest, face to face with God again. This place of rest on earth which the Lord instructed for us, is where we can experience the glory of the Lord, see what He is doing and hear His words on any matter.

In 2 Chronicles 7 it recounts the history of the glory of the Lord entering the sanctuary built by king Solomon. *'The*

Glory of the Lord filled the Lord's house'. This is the shekinah glory cloud of the presence of our amazing, stupendous Lord God. The glorious presence of the Spirit of the Lord Himself can fill our own body/temples.

We can bow down and give Him honour and reverence; bless His holy name! Ask Him to come and fill you with the fullness of His glorious presence. The Holy Spirit of the Lord desires to enter and dwell in the sanctuary of your body and soul. He primarily enters your inner person and longs to transform you from the inside out. His throne is both of great grace and great awe. He has chosen you and me to stand before His throne. His nature is altogether a mystery for us to seek and find.

In a similar way, the Spirit being in us, upon us and at the same time our Spirit being always continually saved and yet needing maintenance is somewhat mysterious. In one sense, your Spirit is already fully made holy and yet He longs to fill you, body and soul with His pure and powerful life.

Be overtaken by the wholeness and wonder of who He is. Thank Him for His in-filling, for who He is, for His love, peace and awe. In His glorious presence may you see a glimpse of His face.

Before the holy priest entered the sanctuary, he first had to make a sacrifice and deal with the people's disobedience (sin). Receiving forgiveness from Jesus and forgiving others is like this sacrifice. It is an important part of our going into the presence of God in worship. In fact, it leads to true worship in Spirit and truth. Cleansing and washing, were also a crucial part of the instructions of God before entering the sanctuary, hence repentance or turning away from evil and asking forgiveness leads to healing in body and mind. We thank you Lord for creating in us a clean heart, and for renewing a right spirit within us.

The meditation on the Word of the Lord in Scripture, the speaking out the truth of Scripture over your body is powerful in enabling freedom from ailments and effects of disobedience:

> *'and we have been healed by his wounds.'*
>
> (Isaiah 53:5)

> *'Those who are planted in the House of the Lord will flourish in the courts of our God. They shall bring forth fruit in old age.'*
>
> (Psalm 92)

In the ancient sanctuary there was a continual presence of unleavened bread set on the table within the holy place, which Father God commanded the priests to commission. It was refreshed each *Shabbat* (Friday evening) as directed by God in Leviticus:

> *And you will take fine flour and bake twelve cakes of it, two tenths of an ephah will be in one cake. And you will set them in two rows, six in a row, on the pure table before the Lord . . .. Every Sabbath he will set it in order before the Lord continually, taken from the children of Israel by an everlasting covenant.*
>
> (Leviticus 24:59)

The bread represents the teaching of Jesus in Scripture through His twelve disciples as there were twelve layers of bread instructed by God to be set on the *'table of showbread'*. As a Christ-follower, a disciple made in His likeness, you have the bread of God's continual presence within you. The bread is representative of God's provision and His nourishing Word to His people. As we digest His Word, we are made holy. The digesting and meditation of His Word is not only head knowledge, but a heart knowledge backed up by experience.

The bread went into the bodies of the holy priests. This indicates to us that we need to take in the Word not only as a study to increase mental knowledge (theology). Just as important is that the Word is *living and active* inside us and therefore causes us to bear the fruit of the Spirit. The bread also represents physical provision of all that we need in the natural.

Your Father in heaven sees you as a holy sanctuary, set aside for Him. He wants you to be healthy spiritually and physically. This is a huge subject, which we shall only touch on here. The instructions Father God gave to Moses in the Bible were common sense life instruction for spiritual and physical well-being.

For instance, He told the children of Israel ('princes of God') what they should and should not eat. He told them not to eat pork for example (Deuteronomy14:8). Nowadays science has proved that pork is full of bacteria and is not the best food for human consumption; this is an example of Father's good instructions which were written thousands of years before the modern scientific era.

The Father is desiring to protect those He loves, to point them to more purified foods such as honey. Honey has been proved one of the purest foods on our earth. Leaves are also implied to be good to eat in the Bible: *'and the leaves of the tree were for healing of the nations'.* (Revelation 22:2). Righteous people are often compared to a tree with flourishing green leaves (Jeremiah 17:8).

God has given us the freedom to choose what to eat because of the newer covenant through His son Jesus. Whilst we need not be offended by each other and our beliefs about food, I believe He has also given us good instructions concerning what is good and what is healing to our bodies. Let us decide to eat wholesome foods, pleasing to God. I have some way to go in this area and am asking for God's help to know balance and be healthy. When we eat well, and take care of our bodies, we are blessed with good health!

> *To the One who loves us and has loosed us from our sins by His blood and made us a kingdom, priests to His God and Father, to Him be the glory and the power forever and ever, amen.*

(Revelation 1:6)

We are a temple where He can meet with us face to face. His full holiness is that which we are not able to see otherwise we will die at the magnitude of His splendour. He showed me that the Holy of Holies within us, is your soul, or your mind and emotions. This type of spiritual representation is very helpful in giving us understanding and revelation of who we are, and a clear picture as to how we are made in the likeness of our Creator.

There is a temple in heaven with a throne room and I believe that our Spirit, body and soul (mind and emotions) are linked through our Spirit to this temple when we are baptised in the Spirit. This connection many call an 'open heaven' which is a continual connection. Jesus answered Nathaniel:

> *'From now on you all will see an open heaven and gaze upon the Son of Man like a stairway reaching into the sky with the messengers of God climbing up and down upon him!'*

(John 1:51)

I have had recurring visions of angels ascending and descending over me. I believe this is an indication of us being a gateway for the heavenly host going up from earth to heaven and back; answering the prayers of the saints and doing the will of the Father. We are like Him in this way. You carry an open heaven over you, as you submit to Father God, through Jesus by the Holy Spirit to bring heaven to earth. We can receive the revelation and authority of who we are in Him. We can live in response to heavens ways.

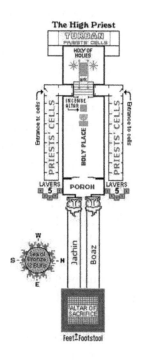

I believe that the temple is a picture of our priestly nature in Him. Below are some of the revelations this can bring:

The ark, which could also be translated as 'the box', is like the mind of Christ; it is also like your own mind. The box was placed in the Holy of Holies and contained the stones on which the words and instructions of God were written; the words given to Moses on Mount Sinai. There were two stones, one of which was smashed. The Holy Spirit showed me that this represents Jesus's smashed body of flesh, and the smashed relationship between mankind and God at the disobedience of Eden.

Moses went up the mountain for a second time and hewed a rock out of Sinai. God wrote the teachings on this second stone. Moses brought it down from the mountain and it was kept in the holy box in the tabernacle sanctuary, along with the smashed stone pieces. Today, Orthodox Jews wear small boxes strapped to their heads to represent the *Torah* (or 'teachings', in Hebrew) that were kept within the ancient ark or box. In Jeremiah, the prophet writes that there will be a new covenant, and that He will put His Torah *'in their inward parts and write it in their hearts'* (Jeremiah 31:3132).

Reading and keeping the Word and teachings of God in your soul (your mind and emotional life) is of great importance in knowing who you are. Knowing the instructions of God and working them out in your life is good for you. Teachings which Father gave you such as keeping the sabbath holy and honouring your parents; following these commands bring blessing to your life. Yeshua, who is Jewish, would have also followed these instructions and what is good enough for Him is good enough for me.

When you surrender your mind to Jesus it is like the blood of the lamb being sprinkled on the mercy-seat of your mind. When you fully realise what Jesus has done for you, and the revelation that His blood sacrifice is sprinkled on the mercy-seat of your mind, you are enabled supernaturally to forgive as He forgave you. Your mind is transformed when you let the blood of His love-sacrifice rest in your mind. Thereafter your heart is nourished and filled with His words and commands.

> *But you must, from the inside, continually be changed into another form, by the renovation of your mind, to prove what is the good and pleasing and perfect will of God for you.*

(Romans 12:1)

You and I can be transformed to have the mind of Messiah Jesus. Jesus wore a crown of thorns upon His head during His ordeal before and on the cross. His head was wounded for the healing of your mind and its transformation, as well being bruised for your iniquity, your sin *'By His stripes you are healed'* and made whole. (Isaiah 53). I understand that there is much more to speak of concerning the health of our minds, so this is a short encouragement for you.

Thank Him for your transformation in faith to be able by His Spirit; to perceive His purposes, from a higher wisdom; from His higher understanding. The transformation of your thought life is very important to your Father. It will help you know who you are.

> *'But we have the mind of Messiah; we know what He has taught.'*

(1 Corinthians 2:16)

It is through communing with the Lord, reading His word, asking His opinion on matters day to day and being aware of His presence that we can *'have the mind of Messiah'*. Ask for His wisdom and understanding as you go about your life.

Father God has highlighted the area of 'mind transformation' as one of the main focuses of change in our lives in these times. God showed me this a few years back as I went on a trip to North Carolina to a 'prayer mountain'. During this holiday we stayed in a log cabin on the top of this holy place. While there we were encouraged to go to a certain cabin in the valley next to us. We were told by a trusted friend that we would experience God's angels gathering there as many others had before us, and that one of them would un-pop my ears to hear what God was saying. It was a prophetic word from God, for sure enough as I sat down to wait, after about five minutes my ears popped! I then heard God through the angel say, 'Romans 12'. At the time I had no idea what was in the text. I now know this scripture well, which speaks of being *continually changed into another form, by the renovation of your mind*.

Let us thank Him for transforming our minds. Let us rebuke all enemy thoughts and strongholds in the mighty authority of Jesus our Messiah, receiving instead His peace and His understanding.

Prayer:

I command every stronghold in my mind that is not of God YHVH to come tumbling down right now!

I rebuke all enemy thoughts of fear, worry, or death in the name of Jesus!

I receive instead peace, joy, and every good way of thinking available.

Thank you, Holy Spirit for renovating my mind anew.

Amen.

Surrendering our bodies and minds is a process, just like physically kneeling down is a process or prostrating ourselves before the Lord in awe (lying face down before God). We are the ones who move ourselves into position.

*Therefore, **if** you would be subject to God, you should resist the devil and he will flee for his life from you.* (James 4:7).

When we take holy action, the enemy flees, and God is magnified in our lives. Christian maturity requires action: *'do what your hand finds to do, for God is with you'* (1 Samuel 10:7 ESV). Your body and mind are a holy temple which needs cleansing each morning and evening so that the Glory of God can rest in us fully. We do this for our bodies, and by connection with Jesus and His Spirit; our souls need similar.

As the psalmist sings: *'to show forth Your loving kindness in the morning and your faithfulness every night,'* (Psalm 92). Daily connection, prayer and worship is a key to being a habitation of the Lord.

In the sanctuary, two cherubim stood guard over the ark and its contents. These angelic beings are very high-up angels who serve God and us. They are messengers from the Lord who are close to Him. I wonder if our minds are guarded by such angels once we belong to God? What a positive thought to think that we may have angels of the Lord guarding our minds.

The actual word 'angel' in Hebrew means 'messenger' which can refer to a divine messenger as well as a physical messenger such as a human/pigeon/dove. Angels do not replace the Holy Spirit; they are servants and messengers who obey the Holy Spirit.

Instead of magnifying negative spirits with your mouth, such as the demonic, you can emphasise God's truth with confidence that you have authority in the heavenlies over them through Jesus. Your focus can be on the good from God, His Word and kingdom in and on yourself. Let us not focus on the evil which tries to cling but focus and commune more with God within you.

'The One, Who is in you, is greater than the one who is in the world'

(1 John 4:4)

When we magnify God in us, we make Him bigger and His Light shines. You are enabled to do all things through the authority of Jesus and through the confidence He gives you. You are His sanctuary, and through faith in Him you have dominion over every evil and every bad spirit. There is wisdom concerning these aspects and I am writing from a faithful viewpoint.

As you develop spiritually, the sanctuary of your earthly body and mind are connected to the sanctuary in heaven. The cherubim which guard the ark or box, can be likened to the wings of the Lord which cover and guard us when we soak in His Spirit and meditate on His Words. It is written:

'He will cover you with His feathers and under His wings you will find refuge; His truth will be your shield and buckler (surrounding guard)'

(Psalm 91:4)

The Passion Translation Bible verse reads: *'we can always come to the place of the mercy seat and rest without fear'*.

We need to be careful of deception concerning the angelic, although we must also not be afraid to study and write about these things, otherwise we lose out on some of Father God's wonders! There are some who focus on the angelic as spiritual guides which replace Holy Spirit. The essential way to overcome this kind of deception is to focus on Jesus and His Word. You can ask for the lover's eyes, or dove's eyes, to read and focus on our Lord Jesus Messiah and His Holy Spirit's beautiful voice and ways.

As you receive by faith the revelation of these aspects of yourself as a sanctuary of the Most High, your whole body is able to be governed and filled with the glory of God Himself. You are a new creation, a brand-new person, when you are re-born into Jesus' saving grace. The sanctuary in 2 Chronicles 7 was filled with the glory of God, and this is how you can be; this is how you can walk the earth bringing the light of the Messiah wherever you move.

This ark or box is also a type of throne that is movable, just like the holy ark of old. In the Torah, God showed Moses how to construct and move the box. Just as the original ark did, the mind can be 'moved' to impact the world around us in terms of a powerful creative way. Following and moving with the Spirit and Word of God enables His Holy presence to fill your temple body and mind. If your temple is full of worldly thoughts and habits, then although He longs to come in, by the nature of His holiness, He is repelled.

The box of our minds is representative of the spiritual throne within ourselves; that which is inside our minds and which literally moves us. When we ask Jesus to be enthroned in our mind, emotions and heart; the Lamb who was slain is seated on that throne. Jesus as the King and the Lion of Judah is on the throne of our life, and He lives within us. When we consciously focus on and magnify Jesus, the dying Lamb and risen Lion can be central to our active lives. This enables us to love as He loves; dying to ourselves and living for Him. Let us have His mind, on our mind.

You are a priest to serve God and are spiritually crowned with eternal life. Instead of wearing a turban made by men, you are crowned with spiritual glory like Jesus, who wore a crown of thorns for your mind to be like His.

You are made in the likeness of God. Being His walking, talking, glorified body, full of His Word, His light and His presence. We are His bride corporately, and we shine brightly as living stones together in Him.

Sanctuary Summary

Seeing the symbolism from the ancient texts can help you know the patterns of how things are created and how they work within you. I am hoping these images help you know who you are. Every *Shabbat,* the priests would make sure the menorah was plied with fresh oil so that it would burn night and day, twenty-four-seven; and that the showbread was freshly placed in two columns of six. In a similar way, you are responsible for surrendering to and maintaining your relationship with Jesus, your high priest; to read and receive His fresh Word and Holy Spirit oil as you worship and rest in Him continually. You and I are responsible for the potential God has placed within us.

In The Holy of Holies, there was a cloud of God's glory present which hovered over the Ark. As you digest His Word and receive the oil of the Holy Spirit into the menorah of your soul, you can know that your mind is full of God's glorious presence. You can ask the Holy Spirit to come and ignite His flame of glory within you, to cleanse you, and shine through you. As you draw upon the Holy Spirit's oils and the 'sap of life' within you, you are transformed from one degree of glory to the next, as the glory of God spills out of your very life to others who come within reach of the 'outer courts' of your body. You are a new creation, a temple of the Holy Spirit in the likeness of your Saviour Jesus.

Let us invite those around us who have not yet experienced His presence, to receive the holy peace from the Spirit of the Lord's light inside of us, as we lay our hands on them. We do so by faith, as priests in Jesus. They are cleansed and healed by God's very presence and power within.

Jesus is the one who makes us Holy. He makes us different from the world. Let us draw upon the Holy Spirit right now. Be aware of your inner person, and relax, and thank the Holy Spirit. Tell Him you love Him, and say, 'I draw upon you'. Breathe in, feel Him filling you up. If you do not feel anything, do not be concerned; do this by faith, and believe that He has filled you with His glory and goodness. He is your breath, your Ruach Ha Kodesh ('Spirit who is holy' in Hebrew). If you want to feel Him, if this is your desire, ask Him, He will help you. Draw close to God and He will draw close to you. Practice, and experience will follow.

Jesus died in this fleshly, worldly place for our disobedience once and for all. He paid a high price so that we could be living, walking, talking, holy sanctuaries to shine out His glory light to those in the world, who will be and are being saved. He is The Light of the world within us. Praise Him!

Prayer:

Lord I thank you that my body is a temple of your Holiness. I repent, I ask your forgiveness and turn away from all that I have done wrong. I also forgive myself. Thank you for making me clean again. Help me maintain this wonderful temple you have given me.

May the temple of my body and mind be continually holy, as You are holy. Make me more like You every hour of every day. I welcome you Spirit of the Lord into my mind, into my whole body.

I am a new creation, and Your Spirit in me has overcome the flesh and the world, that I may live, move and have my being in You every-day.

I ask You, Jesus, to help me magnify all which is good and true. Help me continually focus and magnify You.

Thank You, Lord, that You have faith in me, that You fight for me, that You have saved me, forgiven me.

I thank you for your love and goodness toward me. Fill me now with the knowledge and understanding of who you are and who I am in you Lord through your Word and Spirit.

Thank you that I know you more than I did yesterday and that I am looking more like you today.

My King, rule and reign in my mind and heart.

I honour You, Lion of Judah and Lamb of God.

Lord you are more precious than silver

Lord you are more costly than gold

Lord you are more beautiful than diamonds

Nothing I desire compares with You

Amen!

---

1. The Jesus Discovery. A T Bradford, Adam Bradford, 2010

SEVEN

Menorah

ASK FOR OIL

Be filled with His oil
Drink deep
Draw from the
Holiness of His Spirit
Be ignited
Ask for oil

THE MENORAH is a seven-branched 'candlestick' for which God gave Moses intricate instructions for making:

> *And you will make a pure gold menorah: of beaten work will the menorah be made: its shaft, its branches, its bowls, its knobs, and its flowers will be of the same. And six branches will come out of its sides, three branches of the menorah out of the one side and three branches of the menorah out of the other side.*

> (Exodus 25:31)

I believe this is also significant concerning your identity. There are seven lamps around the throne of God as revealed in Revelation 4:5. These seven are representative of the attributes of the Holy Spirit of God. These attributes link up with the menorah. There's a mystery surrounding these as to whether they are seven spirits or part of the Holy Spirit; people have discussed and believed both. We do know for sure that these seven lamps are at the heart of Father God's nature.

The seven spirits of God are written about in Isaiah 11. This passage is referring to Jesus the Messiah many centuries before He came to earth, and I believe it shows us the likeness of His inner personhood. The menorah is a beautiful picture of the Spirit of the Lord inside us when we are delivered into His loving life and all His attributes shine out from our hearts. I myself believe that the seven spirits around the throne are attributes of the Holy Spirit.

The word *menorah* in Hebrew (which is from *nur*, the verb for 'to flame, shine, give light') reminds me of *torah*, meaning 'teaching, instruction'. As already mentioned, Torah is also a term for the first five books of the Bible, which are a foundation for our faith as Messiah followers. The word *Torah* comes from the Hebrew root word *yarah*, a verb whose various meanings include 'to flow' and 'to throw' and 'to point out'. I see a picture here of the oil flowing through the menorah for lighting the lamps. We can flow with the oil of *Torah*, which the Spirit of Adonai can light up so that our lives are lit with His Spirit and His Word. The Messianic Jewish community believe that Jesus is the walking, talking Torah.

> *And there will come forth a shoot out of the trunk of Jesse, and a Branch will grow out of His roots . . . and the Spirit of the Lord will rest upon Him, the spirit of wisdom and understanding, the spirit of counsel and might, the spirit of knowledge and of the reverence and awe of the Lord.*

(Isaiah 11:12)

In this passage, 'the Spirit of the Lord' is further described as 'spirit' attributes, and together these can be perceived as depicting the seven spirits of the Messiah:

1. the spirit of the Lord;

2. the spirit of wisdom;

3. the spirit of understanding;

4. the spirit of counsel;

5. the spirit of might;

6. the spirit of knowledge;

7. the spirit of reverence and awe of the Lord.

As you are a sanctuary of the Lord, these are inside you, making the light of your life burn brightly. You are a shining one through the powerful Holy Spirit, who is full of the promises of the Father of light and life.

Isaiah 11:2

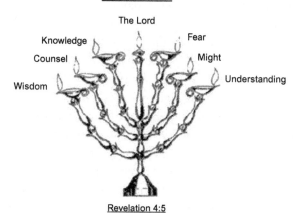

Revelation 4:5

Seven lamps of fire burning before the throne, which are the seven Spirits of God

I have a hunch that the menorah of His attributes resides inside us as it did in the temple. Remember, you are His temple. You can be lit with His oil; full of His Spirit of wisdom, understanding and revelation, counsel, might, knowledge, and awe of the Lord. It is the Holy Spirit who provides the oil to light the flames in our heart and it is our High Priest Jesus who lights these flames. Our part is to maintain the temple of our body, soul and spirit, humbling ourselves to His instructions, His ways, truth and life.

> *Because this revelation lamp now shines within you, nothing will be hidden from you – it will all be revealed. Every secret of the kingdom will be unveiled and out in the open, made known by the revelation light.*

(Luke 8:17 TPT)

In the earthly sanctuary of Solomon, olive oil would have been used, and there is a representation here of fruit being crushed to reveal oil, which lights lamps. Oil in the ancient world was valuable for everyday life, for cleansing, making the face shine, making bread, and for giving light in the darkness. Our Messiah died, having been crushed on our behalf, and His 'oil' (Spirit of life) is poured out into the lamps of our lives so that we shine; so that we can digest His words and bring light to those around us. It is often through trials, suffering and 'crushing', that fruit is formed in our own lives. When we sacrifice ourselves in order to love others; when we 'forget' ourselves for the purposes of serving another; we then manifest His enabling light and sustenance. We display to other people the flames of His love for them.

In the ancient sanctuary, the lamps were continually lit, and it was the priests who were employed to do this every day. This is a reflection of the lamps in heaven around the throne which are eternally burning, and of the lamps which are now alight in your heart. Earth reflects heaven and is 'synchronised' to heaven when your life glows brightly. We pray to our Father; 'May Your Will be done on earth as in heaven'. This pleases your Father in heaven whose desire is for you to display His heavenly glory.

It is your Father's desire that you be continually enflamed with the Holy Spirit burning bright within you. You are then enabled to rule and reign in the light of His pure Spirit with wisdom, revelation, counsel and might, knowledge and awe of the Lord. I believe that Jesus is full to overflowing with all of these attributes and I would like to be more Like Him.

The menorah also represents the tree of life (Genesis 2:9). Trees naturally produce fruit and fruit produces oils to make your face shine; it works the same spiritually when you ask your High Priest Jesus to bless you with more oil of His Spirit. There is a circular truth concerning how the oil is produced. Jesus our Messiah is the vine, and we are His branches. When we abide in Him (when we remain in Him) and in His way, truth and life, we draw sustenance from His roots.

> *The one who dwells in Me and I in him, this one bears much fruit . . .. If you dwell in Me and My words dwell in you, whatever you would wish you must immediately ask, and it will be done for you.*

(John 15:5-7)

I was reminded of the burning bush that Moses saw whilst writing this passage. It was a little tree burning bright with the very light of God himself.

I believe that when we choose to be born-again, we become a new creation in Jesus and are grafted into the tree of life in God's kingdom and can draw from this tree. This holy lamp epitomises the Spirit of Jesus on earth in us. Jesus is the one who is *the* way and *the* truth, and I believe He is the tree of life. He is the Son of God and the son of man, both human and divine. This is a mystery being two things at the same time.

As mentioned previously, there is a wicked 'lamp' tree (see Proverbs 24:20) where we find attributes of abomination to God. Those who seek after God's righteousness and His kingdom do not want these attributes manifesting in their lives. Perhaps when we are critical of others, trusting in ourselves and ignoring God, we are living from the tree of knowledge of good and evil, instead of focusing and drawing from the tree of life.

Good can manifest in us from this tree of testing, but this, in itself is not enough for salvation and transformation. We cannot be transformed inside by our own good efforts; we need the oil of the word and the Spirit of God which is like the sap from the tree of life. Let us draw from this eternal tree. Jesus died on the other cursed tree in order that we may access His heavenly Kingdom and eternal life.

I saw a vision of the menorah lamps alight and there were colours emitted from each light, which arched from one to the opposite lamp like a rainbow coming from the flames. I saw a person fully lit up with colours arching around them in a rainbow 'aura' representing the promises of God and other deep meanings. The rainbow came from the menorah lights which were lit up within their heart. This reminded me of Father God and the rainbow around His throne. We become enthroned in His light and colour which is also our light and colour. As we become more at one with our God, the colours represent His promises in the Bible. When we become bright and beautiful, in word, joy and behaviour, others are drawn to Him and the light of His glory.

Let your body, soul and especially your mind, be full of the knowledge and wisdom of His Word. Draw upon the oil from the Spirit of the Lord's presence and be enveloped in the Holy Spirit fire. Previously, you may have reacted through fleshly emotions, but now that your life is lit by His light and you react with His love. Your life becomes overwhelmed by the true and loving attributes and emotions of His presence. The flames of love produce the fruit of the Spirit: love, joy, peace, patience and more.

There is a tree of life in the heavenly kingdom of God as well as a tree of the knowledge of good and evil (Genesis 2:9). Each tree is different, having its own functions. It is the tree of the knowledge of good and evil that the enemy has used against mankind in order to confuse us.

One of the enemy's main strategies has been to copy or counterfeit that which is holy so that people call what is evil good, and what is good evil. The best way to overcome this is to be grafted into the tree of life. The tree of life can show us how to live righteously, since it is made up of the Word Himself. The menorah is Jesus Himself, as is also the Holy Spirit. Jesus is the light of the world. We are grafted as a branch into their tree. This is a mystery.

God has created the universe with capacity of free choice. This is evident in the Hebrew language, which is rich in choice of positive or negative emphasis. The Hebraic mindset can accept a paradox, two seeming polar opposites to be right and in unity. In Jewish tradition there is a good and bad lamp or menorah. Perhaps this bad lamp is part of the tree of knowledge of good and evil? The bad lamp is described in Proverbs 6:16 where the attributes indicate haughtiness, lying, shedding the blood of the innocent, devising wicked plans, running quickly to do evil, being a false witness, and separating of the brothers and sisters.[1]

Perhaps at times we allow the old enemy who confused Adam and Eve in the garden at the tree of knowledge of good and evil, to influence and confuse us still? Let us ask to see clearly what is rooted in evil through His Word. May we expose evil inside and outside of ourselves by being filled with the light of the Spirit of the Lord which causes evil to flee. It is written, *'whatever revelation-light exposes, it will also correct . . .'* (Ephesians 5:13 TPT). When we surrendered our lives to Jesus, we were grafted into the incredible, eternal tree of life. Let us ask Holy Spirit to remind us who we are. We are a new creation, a brand-new man. We can continually choose to draw daily oil from the spiritual root of life within us. We are grafted into The Light of the World. The Spirit of the Lord enables us to shine bright when we continually choose His eternal reigning resurrection life.

> *See I have set before you this day life and good, and death and evil; . . . I have set before you life and death, blessing and cursing. Therefore, choose life.*

(Deuteronomy 30:15)

Let us not be overwhelmed by our fleshly circumstance or emotion, nor isolate ourselves from God or those who love us. Our Father sees what you are going through, and He wants to share in it and comfort you.

Let us likewise share with Him in suffering and joy together to light up the lamps again, as we identify with Jesus and He with us in our/His suffering. This is a circular movement, which appears all through the *torah* (teaching and instruction) of God. Father God has emotions too and he suffers when he sees the enemy action upon you, His creation. Many have forgotten this aspect of God. Jesus wept as he had compassion on Lazarus and his family when he died. He is a God full of compassion who understands all your weakness and desires to see you whole in Him. He has called you to be an overcomer, to be full of His resurrection, love, power and sound mind.

Prayer:

Thank You Lord, for grafting me into your Tree of Life. Thank you for placing your Spirit within me.

Help me Spirit of the Lord, to have a relationship with, and draw from you daily.

I thank You for transforming me every day, bringing me into another realm of Your glory, to be enabled to show Your light to those in the dark.

You are the Light of the world in me, you shine brightly for those around me. You are my light in the darkness. Thank You, Jesus for keeping my lamp burning until the end.

May I have the wisdom to discern what is evil; to turn away and cling to what is good. Thank you for more clarity and discernment about spiritual things Lord God.

Thank You Lord, for giving me your self-control, especially in the areas of emotional strife I find difficult to bear.

I decide to surrender these situations; these emotions, my whole life to You, Lord.

Thank You Lord, that my fleshly suffering has been turned into the spiritual oils of joy and gladness, and sorrow and sighing must flee away.

Thank You, Jesus, for the vast oil vats of anointing You created on the cross. Thank you for the suffering we have endured which has enabled us to be anointed like You. When we have suffered, yet choose to praise You, or been in a trial and yet choose to praise You; thank you that we shine Your

Light. You turn everything we experience around for good. We thank You Lord for the joy after the trial and for the light You bring to our lives.

Amen.

---

1. *The Creation Gospel* by Hollisa Elwine. www.thecreationgospel.com/resources. The author may not agree with Dr Elwine's entire message.

EIGHT

Be Continually Filled

ANOINTED

He has anointed you
With oils from the fruit
From His garden
Drink deep
From the wine of His delight
Pour out
His love to those
Drawn to His light within
Give Him
Everything

WE EACH HAVE A RESPONSIBILITY, just as the priests of old did, to maintain the spiritual sanctuary within our mind, our emotions, as well as our body.

Worshipping in Spirit and truth enables the oil of the Holy Spirit to fill up the branches of the tree of life (or menorah), which has been placed within you. Coming into His gates with thanksgiving and into His courts with praise is the way to approach our Lord's throne of grace. We can ask Him to create in us a clean heart and to renew a right spirit within us, and we can read His Word, which transforms our minds.

> *Therefore I urge you, brothers, through the compassion*
> *of God, to present your bodies holy, living offerings,*

> *pleasing to God, your spiritual service: and stop*
> *being conformed to this world order, but you must*
> *from the inside continually be changed into another*
> *form, by the renovation (transformation) of your*
> *mind, to prove what is the good and pleasing and*
> *perfect will of God for you.*

(Romans 12:1)

God gave me this scripture whilst on a pilgrimage in North Carolina, to visit the place where the Moravians once settled in the mountains. We went to a beautiful lodge in a valley. There was a small stream bed covered in thousands of gold flecks all along it and we have photographic evidence of this. I asked Father God what the golden 'gravel' was and told me that angels walked along the stream and left their glorious footprints. I sat down as instructed to tune in to what heaven was saying that day, and I heard 'Romans 12:1'. I did not then know what that scripture contained, but it is now one of those that has marked my life. Father was saying that we need to continually present ourselves to Him in order to be transformed from one glory in Him to the next.

Jesus was transfigured and lifted up in Matthew 17. The word 'transfigured' is the same word used in Romans 12 about having a 'transformed' mind. Both Moses, who represents the Torah instruction of God, and Elijah, who represents the prophetic words of God, were with Jesus when he was transfigured. Meditation on the instruction and prophetic words of God in your life is crucial for the transfiguration or transforming of your mind into that which He originally created for you before you were born. Your mind will be full of words of truth which spill out to others as you speak.

Jesus has enabled you to walk and talk with Father God again like Adam and Eve did in the garden of Eden. You can ask the Holy Spirit to come inside and fill you like a well full of living water. Your inner person becomes like a flourishing garden with a fresh well of water in the centre and full of the Holy Spirit of life. You can ask Jesus, the Light of the world to shine down upon your soul and body. It is written that you are like a 'well-watered garden.' (Isaiah 58:11).

May the Lord bless you and keep you and may His face shine upon you and bring you into His peace.' (Numbers 6:24 paraphrase).

Father God wants the serenity of this peaceful place of reality within you to have dominion in your life; to rule over your mind, emotions, and body. Your inner spirit is meant to rule over your other parts. Light and life flood your being when you allow the Holy Spirits' rulership over your entire life. We can make a decision to tell our bodies and minds to be aligned and surrendered to Holy Spirit within the garden of our hearts and He will cause it to flourish with His fruits of love, joy, peace, patience and all the other fruit.

Let us surrender and humble our whole body and mind to His Spirit right now. Speaking in your heavenly language or tongue enables His Spirit in you to overcome your mind, and it is good to do this as much as you can. Remember you can 'speak' in your heavenly language inside of yourself without speech, however it is very powerful as you release Holy Spirits' sounds.

As you walk deeper into the ways of God, you may find that the Holy Spirit talks with you about some things that may be unaligned with heavenly ways; which are unrighteous. If so, simply repent and thank Him for forgiving you. Forgive yourself because you are very much loved and Father God wants you to be free from all hindrance, condemnation and lies of the enemy. He instructed to *'go and sin no more'* in John 8:11. You are to be holy as He is holy. He is quick to forgive when you turn away and look to Him once more. Ask Him to help you and be led not into temptation but delivered from all evil. You have such a great hope of glory ahead of you.

> *Paul says: 'Continually be imitators of me, brothers . . .. fix your attention on those who walk in this manner . . .. You have us as an example . . .. Our citizenship is in the heavens . . .. We have been waiting eagerly for a Saviour for ourselves, Lord Yeshua Messiah, who will transform our body to the same form as His glorious body through the power that enables Him to subject everything to Himself.*

(Philippians 3:17-21)

Why and how are we to maintain this sanctuary we are given? It is in order that you know who you are and be conformed to Jesus's likeness inside and out. Also, so you can go out and extend His rule and reign on earth as it is in heaven. The Word of God says that you need to 'maintain' this sanctuary that He has given you:

> *'Do you not know you are a sanctuary of God and the Spirit of God dwells in you? . . . For the sanctuary of God is holy, which you are.'*

(1 Corinthians 3:16)

Primarily it is for us simply to obey Him and His words. Jesus said that those who love Him obey His commands. (John 14:15) It is written, *'Be Holy, as I AM Holy'* (Leviticus 20:26).

There are several ways to be continually filled. For instance, prayer and asking Jesus to cover you in His blood everyday, keeps your mind, emotions, and body clean. The blood of the Lamb who was slain is sprinkled on the mercy-seat of your mind and emotions as you receive it. Another way is to be filled with the Holy Spirit and to speak in the heavenly language He gives you. This is a powerful tool in transforming your mind.

Personally, the heavenly language I have been given has caused the spiritual atmosphere around me to change. For example, there was a person in front of me manifesting and speaking in a demonic way to me a while back, not making any sense. The person became aggressive. I felt perturbed and afraid. However, when I began 'speaking in tongues' quietly for a while; a physical light came down from above and due to the fact that we were inside, the light was not the sunshine. Holy Spirit gave me courage to speak up and say: 'Jesus is Lord!'. Immediately the person sank down to the floor and returned to their right mind again, which was a relief! The language of the Spirit is powerful.

Intimacy with Jesus is crucial to going deeper and higher in God. He takes us from one level of glory to the next as we focus on all that is good and righteous altogether in Jesus. Spend time with Jesus daily, however you feel, make time to gaze on Him and His Word from your heart. Even though you may not have words of your own, simply looking at Him will help you reflect His love back to you and out to others.

Like the bride in the Song of Songs, we can say to our Bridegroom, King Jesus:

> *As for my own vineyard of love, I give it all to you forever, my beloved one with me in my garden.*

(Song of Songs 8:12 TPT)

Fix your mind on Jesus. Look full into His wonderful face. If you do, you will magnify all that is good and right, both within you and surrounding you.

> *Fix you minds on whatever is true, whatever is worthy of reverence and is honorable and seemly, whatever is just, whatever is pure, whatever is lovely and lovable, whatever is kind and winsome and gracious, if there is any virtue and excellence, if there is anything worthy of praise, think on and weigh and take account of these.*

(Philippians 4:8 AMP)

Worship is a key for being continually filled. In the times of the tribes of Israel, the banner of the Lion of Judah was displayed in worship at the head of the tribes of Israel as they went into battle and war. As you worship in good times and bad, you display this 'victory of faith' banner to the enemy.

Know that you are a prince/princess warrior of God. When you struggle, worship Him as if you already have the victory. His banner is already victorious through the cross, His name is YHVH Nissi (the Lord your banner of victory and miracle working power).

In the Bible, the tribe of Judah would also to go before all the tribes of Israel as they travelled. Judah means 'Praise'. 'Praise' continually went ahead of the nation, especially when they went to battle. This is a key to overcoming in life.

Again, worshipping Father, Jesus and the Holy Spirit is a key to remaining clean and overcoming your enemies. There was a time when I went to worship Father God even though I was feeling poorly and could not speak or sing due to a virus. Instead of sitting and accepting this situation, I arose and danced in the spirit like a child at the back of the meeting. When I sat down, we were asked to greet one another, so I turned to greet the person next to me and I was able talk once more! My voice was fully healed, and the Spirit of the Lord had discarded the virus from my body as I worshipped! Wow! God is very good.

Loving our Father God and putting Him first in your life is another key. This is His first instruction to us: '*You will have no gods before me*' (Exodus 20:3) and '*Love the Lord your God with all your strength*' (Mark 12:30). We become like the one we love and worship.

This is a growing love relationship. We are going to investigate some of the ways to grow our relationship with the Father in the next few paragraphs.

You can practice being aware that He is with you constantly. Just as the children of Israel followed the cloud in the desert, so also you can follow the presence of Jesus Himself. Stop what you are doing for a moment and be aware of the unseen realm; that which is inside you. What is God saying in your heart? Is Jesus in the room with you? Are messengers there who have come to give you a message from Father's throne of grace?

You can be in the habit of doing this every day. I practiced this recently and felt the words: 'He is Love, He is Light in the Darkness' which led into a worship song, which in turn focused my being on magnifying God. Write down the words you hear and make a habit of this. It is a valuable habit to cultivate. Reflect on what you hear from God from time to time and it will build up your faith. This book is a result of these habits.

Spending time with Father and Jesus in worship, prayer and His Word enables you to be filled to overflowing with Him. He is in you and you are in Him.

You are accepted by and in the Beloved. You can trust in the saving grace of the Son of God. Because of His sacrificial love, because He has suffered and overcome suffering, shame, death, and all evil just for you; you can trust what He says. He encourages you to surrender completely to His love.

Inspired by Father God, Paul wrote:

> *For I have betrothed you to one Husband, to present you a chaste virgin to Christ . . . I appeal to you, therefore, and beg you, in view of all the mercies of God, to make a decisive dedication of your bodies – presenting all your members and faculties – as a living (loving) sacrifice, holy and well-pleasing to God.*

(2 Corinthians 11:12 & Romans 12:1 NKJV)

I have wondered in the past about how I can move more fully into all that He has for me? I have found that a good place to begin is to be aware of living and moving and having my being in Him. You can take every step of your day in God, being aware of Him. It is a choice to live and have your being in God. We need to choose well every day and even every moment. The more we practice, the brighter we become in Him and Like Him.

For instance, when you put cream on your face or wash your face in the morning, you can thank Him for anointing you with His oil of joy and of peace; of royalty and priesthood. When you open a door, you can thank Him for opening doors for you in terms of opportunities, jobs, people, or places. You can thank God for the open door He has placed for you in heavenly realms. When you climb stairs, you can thank God for His heavenly realms and that He takes you from one level of glory to the next in Him, so that you are saturated in Him. When you sit down you can do so in awareness of resting in Him and ruling with and in Him. You are able to live seated with Him, to rule and reign from heavenly realms, declaring His heavenly words on earth.

When you walk forward, by faith you can walk from this world into God's kingdom, to see what Father and Jesus and the Holy Spirit are doing. When you make something to eat, you can chat to the Holy Spirit about it. When you work, you can bring God into whatever you do, you can focus you soul and heart on God in all you do. If it is a menial task, this should be easier; you can speak in your heavenly language and worship as you go along.

When you bathe or shower, you can sing out in worship or pray quietly or silently. God hears our thoughts and silent prayers, and He delights in them. You can thank God for His cleansing power and love and can delight in Him. Similarly, when you dress, you can do it by faith and thank Him for His 'robes of righteousness'. Put on all the armour of God as you ready for the day.

Working in a more complex job, you can give the task to the Holy Spirit before you begin, thanking Him for His help and guidance. I am now thanking God that He has saved me even when I 'save' my work on the computer! It is fun!

I have heard other more mature followers of Jesus say that it is possible to do a task on earth and be in heavenly realms at the same time.

In his book 'The Practice of the Presence of God, Brother Lawrence writes: 'the soul's eyes must be kept on God . . . when something is done in the outside world . . . it is the heart whose attention we must carefully focus on God'[1].

Who is this wonderful God we serve? For this is also who *you* are made to be like.

Honouring our Father God in giving testimony is another way forward toward a deliberate change of mind and heart. Father is so glad to be honoured and known for the good things He is doing. Even small things, in fact, especially the small things. You can make a conscious effort to testify to your family, to your friends, and to strangers about what He has done for you today.

My husband and I run a small business, and I have many testimonies about God's faithfulness and help. For example, I am responsible for recruitment, and I could not find the candidate we needed over many months. I gave up my own efforts after some hard trying. One day I decided to say a quick prayer: 'Help, Lord! Do You know anyone who would fit the bill?' God answered straightaway with a specific name. I was in the car at the time, so when I got home, I typed in the man's name in our recruitment database. Lo and behold, the chap was just the type of candidate I was searching for. I called him on the phone, and he was searching for a new position! Now this man works for us and his life has been changed for the better ever since. God is so good; He is also a good matchmaker.

God always helps in our journey to be whole again. It is in knowing our Father God, Jesus and His Spirit; being with Immanuel that you will know complete wholeness in yourself. He is the Prince of peace, and you are made in His likeness. He wants you to live from this place of peace, of shalom.

Another way that I get to know God more is through visions and I believe this is also available to all God's children. In one such vision that occurred over many days, Holy Spirit took me to a peaceful lake. We went there again and again; it is called Peace Lake. I got to know how strong Jesus is in this place. I love His strength; He has strong arms. I knew Him there as a builder, creator, and betrothed beloved, all at the same time.

In the vision He sanctified me and baptised me in the water of the lake, head and all. He wrapped a big white blanket around me. After this, we went to Father God's throne room where I was dressed in a blue dress, and a sparkling red robe was put on my shoulders. I am told that this is for authority and might, and the blue was for revelation.

I then bowed before my Father God and before Jesus, and Jesus 'knighted' me with a sword. I arose and He placed a chunky pendant necklace over my head. It was a smaller version of a priest's breastplate, with twelve jewels upon it in His chosen colours. It was a more rounded shape and not that of the high priest's breastplate, but 'priestly' nevertheless. He has made us all priests and kings to serve Him on earth and by faith you and I are looking more like Him today than yesterday. You can ask Him to see clearly and for dreams and visions. They enable us to know more fully who we are in Him.

Being a priest and a king of the Most High God means that we are born into a new kingdom. The kingdom of the heavenlies is our home. Just as the sanctuary is in heaven, so are we.

In Matthew 25, Jesus speaks of the kingdom of the heavenlies as being like ten virgins. Five were wise and five were foolish. The wise ones had purchased oil for their lamps and were prepared for the Bridegroom when he came at a delayed hour. These wise ones are representative of walking heavenly habitations of the Most High God. Although this parable speaks of 'virgins', these are representing both male and female genders on earth. The wise ones received the Spirit of Jesus and invested in being continually filled. As for those who did not have oil to light the lamps of their hearts and to shine out His glory, they were not being a heavenly habitation of God on earth; not hosting His presence.

Let us not be like the five foolish virgins who were not intentional about being filled with His Holy Spirit continually. They were told by Jesus:

'Truly I say to you, I do not know you.'

(Matthew 25:12)

The number ten in the Bible also is quite often used for tests; for instance, the ten plagues of Egypt, or the ten talents. Perhaps the maintaining of the holy lamp within ourselves is a test from Father God. It is a test to remain in a place of being full of Holy Spirit glory and grace; to be a light for others and to show the glory of God on earth. Perhaps you are being fully 'you' when this is happening. When you are full of His kingdom glory, you are a doorway from heaven to earth to bring about healing, miracles, and life, just as Jesus did when He was on earth.

The Lord spoke to me about another aspect of how to be filled continually with Him and to overcome. This is by way of *mikvah* (immersion). The Israeli person ritually immerses themselves at certain times; in our culture we call it a bath! I have noticed that I hear God much more easily either while bathing or afterward; it has been a place of 'soaking' and listening to Him. This is due to the fact that I do this by faith; faith in the knowledge that I have repented on many occasions and been forgiven and have also forgiven others; leaving these past happenings and difficulties in the waters. You can rise from the waters of a bath leaving a load behind you. This is not a ritual done with a spirit of religion but an act of intentional devotion in and by the name of Jesus. This can be experienced by both men and women. Both temple priests as well as men and women in the Bible, took part in a similar 'ritual' and of course baptism is a powerful act we are instructed to do in the new testament as part of our salvation journey.

The word for waters in Hebrew is *mayim,* and the word for the heavens is *shemayim.* Water is linked to the heavenly kingdom of God. If you feel distant from God, try having a bath along with playing some 'soaking worship music'. Instrumental is best as this allows your mind to rest in Him and to hear Him more readily.

Here are a couple of poems I wrote and a vision I had after having a soaking time in the Lord:

Safe

I am safe
In this place from
All trials and tests
At rest
Where His
Clouds cover
Like a garment
Enemies blinded.
His fire chased away
The ravening wolves.

Streams

The kindness of spring and autumn rain
Gentle and kind
Gentle and kind
Is the waterfall
Sound of His love for you
Rivers rise carving
Streams of sound
Into earth and marsh
Until now,
When the rushing rise spills out
Cleansing and healing
Giving out the Father's
Love wherever it goes
We bathe and play in its streams.

I had a vision from God whilst soaking in His presence. Jesus, the Messiah of all the world, came to me. He opened up His heart and drew out of His chest a jar of honey. He told me to taste and eat. I received the jar and had an instinct to feed Him with a spoon that had just appeared. As soon as I fed Him a spoonful, the jar of honey grew three times as large. He was pleased and fed me in return. After He fed me, I could see that the effects were good, going down deep within me and healing me. Ever since this vision, I was asked to pray for several people to have revelations of Jesus himself – they all received more of His Spirit. He is the Word of life.

I was given this scripture a couple of days later:

> *'But you, son of man, Listen! Obey what I Am says to you! Do not be rebellious like that rebellious house! [I have learned that this means those who are disobedient to God.] Open your mouth and eat what I Am gives you.' And when I looked, behold, a hand was sent to me and lo a scroll of a book was there. And He spread it before me . . . Moreover, He said to me, 'Son of man, eat what you found. Eat this scroll and go speak to the House of Israel.' So, I opened my mouth and He caused me to eat that scroll. And He said to me, 'Son of man, cause your belly to eat and fill your belly with this scroll that I give you.' Then I ate it and in my mouth it was as sweet as honey.*

> (Ezekiel 2)

Reading, meditating and remembering the Word of God is one of the primary ways to be continually filled.

For truth (God's Word) is a bright beam of light
shining into every area of your life, instructing and
correcting you to discover the ways to godly living.

(Proverbs 6:23 TPT)

When you 'feast' on His word, remember and hold His Word in your hearts, you have received wisdom and understanding of how to live. It is a wonderful adventure of discovering the truth of who He is, which lasts your whole earthly life!

Communion throughout the day is a powerful way to build relationship with the Lord. It enables a remembrance of the awesome act which our Saviour chose to do for us. It reminds us that the veil has been torn away from our eyes and that Father God's heavenly kingdom is close by.

You are enabled to commune with our Father in heaven once more, since His Son died and rose again on our behalf. Jesus' blood has blotted out your sin. He has covered you with His love once and for all.

Recently I have been taking communion more often. Some weeks I take it every day or more than once per day. I am finding that as I walk this life of awareness of and in God, the Holy Spirit will remind me to take communion. Smith Wigglesworth, the great miracle worker, used to take communion often. Perhaps this was one key to his success for healing and miracles? I take communion by myself at present, but sometimes I invite others. I am full of faith and am encouraged in my faith when I undertake this wonderful and mystical act. I have noticed that I have not been ill much during the time that I have been taking communion regularly and I believe that this due to the body and blood of Jesus at work in my body. '*By His Stripes I am healed*' (Isaiah 53). Perhaps you can see what happens when you also do this.

Everything is possible as you welcome Him into every part of your life. A key is that we continually surrender our lives to God, for the sake of becoming and belonging to Him.

The whole point of being continually filled is to serve others because this delights our Father in heaven. Do to others what you would like to be done to you is also God's nature.

I had an insight whilst reading about the parable of the pearl of great price, which is a picture of who you are and how being like Him helps other people. God showed me that you are like a beautiful pearl in God's hands; a pearl of great price that was bought by Jesus on the costly cross. The Holy Spirit showed me that pearls are a sign of being a gateway. The Bible indicates that the heavenly gates of God's kingdom are made of huge pearls. When you know Jesus and the spirit of wisdom, your light is constantly bright with His wisdom. You are like a pearly gateway for others to come into His heavenly kingdom.

A pearl can be made through grit getting inside the shell. The grit is the trial which, when overcome by focusing on God and being filled, becomes shiny instead of dull. Trials can be all sorts of things: financial, health, expansion, family etc. When we rely on God instead of our own strength it is through the supernatural overcoming power of God that we can overcome the grit trials in our lives. He is honing us into being His beautiful pearl-white gates to bring others into His kingdom of heavenlies.

Another aspect of the pearl revelation is that Jesus himself is the main pearl who suffered and through the grit of His earthly life and His suffering, He has become an overcomer for you. Jesus himself is a gateway, a precious pearl, and knowing Him and going through Him as the gateway is a key to knowing who you really are. The more you know Him and yourself, the more you are enabled to love others and impact the world for good.

Let us desire to be the wise ones who are continually filled with the oil of the Holy Spirit and the Word of the Lord. This means being intentional about reading the Bible and spending time with God, whatever that looks like. It might mean soaking and listening/seeing visions; worshipping alone or with others; turning our thoughts towards heaven in the daytime and being aware of His presence with us by faith; praying alone or with others; taking communion and appreciating His creation. There are so many ways to be continually being filled. Let us prioritise this as we await and be a tree branch continually full of His oil.

Prayer:

Teach me how to walk in your presence Lord, how to go about my day in Your Way.

Come in and fill my body, soul and heart, Spirit of the Lord; cause me to produce Your flowers and thereafter fruits of goodness and compassion.

Help me to be continually filled and aware of your presence for in your presence is where I belong.

Thank You, Holy One, for being in my heart. I draw upon Your anointing inside. Light the flames in my heart so that I burn with the fullness of all the attributes of the likeness of You!

Give me oil in my Lamp, keep me continually burning for You, Your Way, Truth and Life.

Amen.

---

1. The Practice of the Presence of God, Whitaker House, USA 1982

NINE

Adam and Ishah

FINAL FEAST

A part of Your beautiful holy bride
Set apart for the I AM
Inviting others to become one with You
Spirit, show me
How to make garments of glory
Ready for Your return
Thank You for the gift of You
Thank You for Your blessings of oil and wine
And the table in the midst of battle
As the trumpet sounds
We invite all to proceed
To the ceremony of all ceremonies
In our together place
And the final feast

IN THE BEGINNING, Adam was formed from the earth; his name means 'earth'. Adam was to have dominion over it, as caretaker especially of the garden called Eden, meaning delight. Before Eve was taken out of him, Adam is believed by Hebrew scholars and Christians to incorporate both male and female, or better put, the whole of humankind.[1]

He was created in the likeness of God himself who has both male and female attributes. After this in Genesis 2 Eve was made as Adams' help, as God saw that it was not good for Adam to be alone. Like the animals, they too were given names: *Ishah* or wife in English and *Ish* or husband.

> *'And He built the rib . . . this is now bone of my bones and flesh of my flesh. She will be called Wife (Ishah), because she was taken out of Husband (Ish). Therefore, a man will leave his father and his mother and will cling to his wife, and they will be one flesh'*

(Genesis 2:22-23 – emphasis added)

It is at the point of separation of Adam and Eve that the male and femaleness of gender became distinct. The two however, were to be still 'of one flesh'. Adam and Eve were to be fruitful and multiply all that was good.

The picture in Genesis 2:22-23 is beautiful. As I read it and applied it metaphorically to the bride and Jesus, our bridegroom, I can see the picture of His bride being 'built' by our creator God, which is the word used in the text.[2]

Let us look a little more closely at the bride of the Messiah. In spiritual terms, when you chose to belong to Jesus; in spiritual terms you become *'Ishah'* (wife) or 'betrothed one'. The two are 'one', but at the same time are also two, much like an earthly marriage. The fullness of the bride is revealed in the Kingdom of God at the end of the age as depicted by John in the book of Revelation.

When you are baptised, you are 'resurrected' into the likeness of Jesus and become a new betrothed creation in His Kingdom. You belong to Him. Obviously, this is true for both men and women who are *in* the 'bride of Messiah'. The bride is without earthly gender; she is a spiritual bride. She is a holy nation belonging to God's Kingdom and in heaven there is no marriage in terms of the flesh; but the marriage is spiritual between The Lord and His betrothed. These are spiritual revelations of which I write.

This word *ishah* also means a military ally, one who protects; an equal helper. It is also a picture of who the Holy Spirit is. The Spirit is feminine in the ancient biblical texts and is hidden like the wind, for instance, the description of wisdom in Proverbs 8 is feminine: *Sophia* meaning 'wisdom'.

From the Hebraic perspective, we see the man as representing Father God and the woman representing the Spirit of God throughout the scriptures, particularly the Old Testament. This explains how women are more 'hidden' within and 'inside' the biblical text, and men appear more outwardly, through loving, kind behaviour. The two genders together make wholeness in the breathed Word of God.

Whether a man or woman, you can be the inward expression of Jesus's holy *ishah* ('wife', or 'betrothed'), and this will reflect in your life outwardly.

Much has been spoken in our gatherings about the role of the Father, and it is important to speak also concerning the crucial role of the inward workings of the Holy Spirit. The Spirit of the Lord brings liberty to captives and enables the healing miracle working power of the Lord to be manifested on earth like in heaven.

When men and women come together as His bride in unity, the circle is completed and we become like our 'last Adam' (we become like Jesus spiritually by faith, Jesus-spiritually neither male nor female, but simply one with Him). Jesus is the 'last Adam'[3] and we take His name as our own when we are betrothed to Him.

> *'The first man was Adam in living life', the last Adam has become a life-giving spirit'*

> (1 Corinthians 15:45)

Father God did not want a robotic slave to look after His creation. This is shown by Him giving Adam a choice and a test, to freely eat from all the trees except one, *'but you will not eat of the tree of the Knowledge of Good and bad'.* (Genesis 2:17) God ultimately gave all of us a choice and a test.

Just like in the garden of Eden, our choice is still a big aspect of who we are and who we become. When you choose and submit to Jesus and His way you become a new creation. Salvation is not just a one-time happening, but it is on-going; us 'being saved'.

Just like the name of God, 'I AM being who I am being', you are continually being a new creation and moving closer and closer in likeness to His righteousness and goodness.

God was not lonely and so He made you, rather He loves your company. Because Adam and Eve made the worst of choices, so Father God sent the last Adam (Jesus) to enable this new ongoing creation to happen in you. Jesus is the meaning behind all the promises and words already written in the Scripture. He was sent as a new creation to earth, but this time born from heaven.

I have a hunch that we, as the 'being built' bride of Christ, are a type of a 'last Eve'. Spiritually speaking; 'man and woman' are the new creation. This bride is made holy and righteous through the saving grace of our bridegrooms' love.

I believe that being a part of the bride means to focus on Jesus himself and His words, for He is the one who we are to be like the most. It is good to be single-minded.

There is an encouraging teaching about the meaning of the word 'Passover' which is *Pesach,* in Hebrew. *Pesach* means 'hopping' like a lamb.

> *'How long will you dance between two opinions? If the LORD is God, follow Him, but if Baal, follow him'.*

> (1 Kings 18:21)

Let us not *hop* between two opinions because when Jesus died on that cross as our *Pesach* lamb, all His 'hopping' came to an end. Jesus gave up his own opinion, submitting to His Fathers will. He hopes we will choose to receive His single-minded love sacrifice and choose His truth.

We are to act on his command to '*love one another as I have loved you*' (John 13:34) to 'go heal the sick, cast out demonic' and 'raise the dead' (my paraphrase). Let us choose God's truth via His Word in our lives.

In His death and life, we can have strength to stop this hopping between our own opinion and God's. There are many opinions which seem Godly but are nothing to do with God's word. It is good to ask yourself – what does God's word say on this matter? For instance, it is written, . . . concerning the Bride of Christ, in Revelation 21:9 '*Come I will show you the beautiful bride, the wife of the Lamb*'. John then describes a beautiful city of peace in which the sanctuary and shining light is the Lord God himself. It is a wonderful picture of our glorious home to come, where we will be corporately one with God, living in Him perfectly and completely.

It may be good to emphasise this finality when thinking about the church on earth in its present state. There has been so much division and yet the spiritually speaking this is how we look in the 'I will be who I will be' generation; in the future. In His name, by faith, we are one.

Covenant with Jesus – You Belong to Him

When we give ourselves fully to Jesus by being born again and being baptised by immersion and Holy Spirit fire, we are cutting covenant with Jesus and Father God, and He is cutting covenant with us. Maybe you need to have deeper revelation of who you belong to?

Intimacy with Jesus is a key to being filled with the fullness of His presence. He shares who He is with you and you share who you are with Him; He accepts you and makes you continually His.

The ancient deep ritual of covenant is in the Bible and shows us meaningfully who we are as a new creation person. Think of how the following may apply to you:

- The covenanted persons exchange names. You are a *Christ*ian (a Christ-one) who belongs now to Jesus. Jesus has given you His name, just as a husband gives his wife his last name when they marry.

- The covenanted one becomes part of a new tribe or nation. You now belong to the kingdom of the Heavenlies, Jesus's unseen realm and domain and not the world's system, culture or domain.

- Covenant parties cut themselves and draw blood. A scar is formed to remember that they belong to each other. Likewise, Jesus has scars, which show He has promised Himself to us. He will not be healed of those scars since they are a sign to His Father and to you, of His absolute commitment. Let us give our lives to Him, as He has given His to us. We remember our covenant together by taking the bread and wine He instructed us to take.

When we cut covenant with God, by giving ourselves to Him, it is an awe-inspiring happening. We are 'betrothed' to Jesus as His bride. We walk out this betrothal to Him throughout our lives.

When two people marry, they make a blood covenant, which is why divorce is so painful. True marriage, as defined by the Bible, is not simply words or a 'contract', even if the husband and wife believe that.

When we promise ourselves publicly to Father God through Jesus, we are covenanting with Him, and through His blood we are 'betrothed' to Him. In ancient times the betrothal was as binding as the full marriage vow. However, this is unlike an earthly betrothal; we are as spiritual beings in His kingdom.

Jesus taught, I believe, that we are without the boundaries of earthly gender restriction in His kingdom. Betrothal to Jesus is with a heavenly kingdom husband; a spiritual spouse. This means whether male or female, if you have covenanted with Jesus, you are part of His betrothed bride. His blood was shed for you once and for all; It is finished! Jesus' blood is both divine and earthly and over-rides the bloodshed of the shameful behaviour of our ancestors, as well as our own wrongdoing, which is sin.

The word in Hebrew for blood is sounded out as: 'dam'. The word for 'blood' is in the name of A-dam. The first Adam fell, and blood was thereafter spilt on the ground. Jesus our Bridegroom, the 'last Adam', poured out His spotless blood for us. The Scriptures say that *Life is in the blood*. Jesus is your powerful saving 'life blood'.

God instructed how to kill an animal in the Bible as an offering to cover the sin of the people. He instructed the priests to pour the blood onto the earth, instructing them how this was to be done. The name 'Adam', in Hebrew means 'earth'. Your Saviour, Jesus poured out His blood onto the Earth/Adam. He poured out His blood onto you, me and all creation for an offering for our sin and disease once and for all. By His wounds you are healed and by His blood poured out you are delivered from Father's anger against your disobedience.

The *ancient* Hebrew wedding covenant is a picture of the process of who we are when we give our lives to Him. Below are some of the steps. This is a picture of your own life and the process that has happened, and is happening, during your transformation into Jesus's kingdom family:

- The father sends out a matchmaker or goes himself to choose a bride for his son.

- The father gives a gift of gold and treasure (see Genesis 24:53) to the bride-to-be, so that others may know also about the betrothal. A betrothal is a binding agreement. (Jesus gives us not only silver and gold, but the gift of His whole life – 1 Peter 1:18-19).

- The bride-to-be accepts the fathers' gift as a sign of her desire to be married or betrothed. In ancient tradition, the betrothal was as important as the wedding ceremony, and one needed a divorce in order to break the engagement. (Messianic Jews also look at the instructions of God in His Word as the treasure).

- The bride and groom write out their *ketubah* or written agreement of terms. They then shared a cup of covenant wine to seal their agreement. (For us, the ketubah is the living Word of God, and we can write or speak out our devotion back to Him in our worship).

- The Bride receives further gifts from the groom to remind her of his coming to marry her. (In her book, 'The Ancient Jewish Wedding' Jamie Lash writes: 'gifts of the Holy Spirit are like precious jewels which adorn Messiahs bride', see Ephesians 1:13-14).

- The two experience *mikvah* (being fully immersed in water) and become cleansed. (Jesus went through baptism on earth, and we follow Him in full immersion, or *mikvah)*.

During the betrothal time of around a year, the groom would prepare a home in the house of his father for the new couple to begin their married life together. (Jesus has gone to His Father's house to prepare a place for us). The bride would prepare her wedding garments during this time and consecrate herself to her husband. The betrothed were considered married, although the marriage had not been consummated. The second part of the marriage now ensued:

- The bride and groom knew the approximate time the groom would come for her, but it was the father who gave his final say when the marriage was to begin and so there was a great element of surprise in the waiting. (Matthew 25:1-13).

- The time of arrival was a surprise since the father was the one to decide the timing, and so the bridal party were always to be ready. (Matthew 24:32-36). A trumpet would be sounded at the beginning of the wedding. The entire wedding processional would then go out onto the streets of the city at the sound of the trumpet. It was the custom for friends of the groom to go ahead and lead the way to the bride's house, shouting 'Behold the Bridegroom comes!' (1 Thessalonians 4:16-18).

- The bridegroom would go to the Fathers house in ancient times, where they would set up the *chuppah (home taking, room or covering)*. The bride would have been carried there on a palanquin originally (Song of songs 3:9-10). The couple then stand under the chuppah, a sign of their dwelling together in unity and of their new home. Nowadays, this is symbolised by a canopy. The betrothed couple would be blessed over a cup of wine to seal the vows made publicly. (this maybe why Jesus lifted-up the wine of the new covenant for us as a seal of promise to His bride).

- In ancient times they would then consummate the marriage. (Song of Songs 2:4 'He bought me to the banqueting house and His banner – or 'chuppah' – over me is love.')

- This was followed by seven days of feasting and celebration (Revelation 19:79).

For more precise information on the process described above please refer to: 'The Ancient Jewish Wedding' by Jamie Lash, Jewish Jewels 2012.[4]

Prayer:

We thank You, Father God of our heavenly kingdom, for Your awesome and wonderful plan for the whole of history.

Thank you that we are your desired Bride for your beloved only Son.

Thank you Jesus, our bridegroom that you have prepared a place for us in Your Kingdom and that You are coming soon.

Amen.

Jesus is currently preparing a heavenly place for us and so should we be preparing the sanctuary of our bodies, minds and spirits, consecrating our lives to the Lord. Father God wants a healthy bride for His son. Ask God to continue to accelerate the process of the transformation of your mind to become fully part of the spiritual bride of Messiah: becoming holy and spotless. Being Holy as He is holy.

You are already a new creation as you stand by faith in His Word. We can pray for our earthly bodies to be transformed and healed to be in alignment with your spirit, this is the will of Jesus and is evidence that we are already more like Him.

If you are lacking in any way physically or emotionally let us pray and believe for health and healing for you. *'By His stripes you are healed'* (Isaiah 53). He wants you to be fully whole and one with and In Him.

Prayer:

Thank you for your Word which says: *'I shall put none of these diseases upon you . . . for I AM the Lord who heals you'*. (Exodus 15-26)

Thank you, Lord that you are coming for a spotless healthy holy collective bride; we look forward to your return whilst watching and waiting patiently.

We desire to please you, help us be holy like you.

The Spirit and The Bride say 'Come Lord!'

Amen.

The Soldier Bride

We are His bride collectively, and we are in a war during our betrothal time. We therefore must be soldiers; a warrior bride. We are equipped with full-battle regalia in this time. Ephesians 6 shows us we are to take up the sword of the Spirit, which is the Word of God, as well as the belt of truth, the breastplate of righteousness, the helmet of salvation, and the gospel of the peace of our bridegroom. It is always in, and with love that we battle the forces of evil, since there is no law against love! This is a real battle against the unseen world and the forces of darkness. The difference with this battle is that our bridegroom, the Son of Love has won already. Our battle is to enforce this loving kingdom victory on earth as it is in the heavenlies.

Prayer:

Lord, we thank you of the armour you have provided for us. We praise you for Your protection around us according to your Word.

We thank you that you have made us man and woman to complement each other. We thank you Father that you saw Adam and Eve, male and female and blessed them declaring everything in your creation to be: 'very good!' (GEN 1:31 NKJV).

Thank you, Holy Spirit for Your continual filling of oil. We thank you for the transformation you have and are doing on us and in us, to make us more like Jesus. Thank you that you are Spirit and *'and where the Spirit of the Lord is, there is freedom'*. We all, by raising the veil, are transformed from glory to glory by the Spirit of the Lord, to behold the glory of the Lord. (2 Corinthians 3:1718).

We look forward to Your coming by surprise. We remain ready and full of the oil of the Holy Spirit, by faith; who you have left with us; the greatest gift we have!

We are so eagerly looking forward to tasting the wine of blessing in your kingdom, and we thank you for the wine already tasted. We are tending our garments and we ask for your help in making them beautiful. Thank you for your adornments that you bestow upon us, your bride.

We are loving going out and showing everyone in the land who you are, and that we are betrothed to be married soon, once and for all; the marriage feast will be glorious just as You are!

We are looking forward to seeing who you have invited to the final feast, Father, and celebrating our covenant with Jesus and our new kingdom family. Thank you for helping us whilst we wait.

Amen.

New Covenant Meaning

As a bit of fun, I have included the names of the books of the newer covenant. In my journey with God, I have found that delving into the meaning of a name is insightful for the rest of the following scripture passage. A name usually describes the character of the person, city or nation.

In this case, the names and their meanings show a beautiful picture of us collectively as the bride and of the Messiah himself. He wants us to be one with him and so the meanings can be applied to both us as his bride and to Jesus. This is the description of the true bride of the Messiah.

Here is the list of names and their meanings. I have personalised them so you can speak them over yourself as a declaration of who you are in Him:

Matthew:	you are a gift to God/a gift of God, you are honouring to God/honouring of God
Mark:	you are servant of God
Luke:	you are luminous; peaceable
John:	you are full of grace; humble
Acts:	you have the ability to perform; be powerful
Romans:	you are full of strength, vigour, sturdiness
Corinthians:	you are satisfied, beauteous, ornamented
Galatians:	you are pure, courageous
Ephesians:	you are wanted/desirable
Philippians:	you have strength, speed, powerful movement; transformed

Colossians:	you are one who brings correction/does not tolerate disobedience (not tolerating sin)
Thessalonians:	you are victorious (over sin and all its affects)
Timothy:	you are honouring God, honourable
Titus:	you are a giant in the kingdom of God/ a firebrand
Philemon:	you are worshipful to God, intimate with God,/kiss Him/affectionate with God
Hebrews:	you are 'one from the other side' or one who has 'crossed over' onto the other side; you are one who seeks after the kingdom of the heavenlies and its righteousness and not of the world; you are set apart (OT imagery is of those who crossed Jordan into the Promised Land)
Jacob:	you are a supplanter (you supplant the enemy Satan; you crush his head with your heel – Jacob caught hold of Esau's heel)
Peter:	you are a rock, reliable and firm (you stand on Jesus, your 'rock of salvation' so that you are a 'rock of salvation' to others)
John:	you are full of grace
Jude:	you are full of praise; and to be praised in terms of pleasing to God and man
Revelation:	you are the bride unveiled (to the world) and the Messiah is hidden within you.

All the names of the New Testament build a picture describing some of the attributes of who you are individually and collectively as His bride. How wonderful.

1. 'The term Adham is again the meaning of humankind, Hebrew thought seldom separated the physical from the spiritual and visa-versa but the whole of humanity is wholly entirely considered. It is the whole human that was created in the image and according to the likeness of God.' The Beauty in The Womb-man, Rhonda Elaine Carroll, iUniverse, 2004.
   'Then God said, *We will make mankind*' (note: the word 'mankind' is Adam in Hebrew (Strongs 120). Used here means man or mankind, the same way that man in English can refer to one person or to all mankind. That he made both male and female indicates that He was speaking of all mankind.)' Genesis 1:26
2. The Hebrew word 'Banah' is used of the word concerning eve which means to build (Strong's H1129)
3. https://creation.com/first-adamlast-adam
4. The Ancient Jewish Wedding, Jamie Lash, Jewish Jewels, 1997.

TEN

Sons and Daughters, Kings and Priests

EMOTIONAL

Whisper in your Father's ear
Thankfulness and truth
Tell Him what He means to you
He has feelings too
Tell Him of your hearts desire
He cares so much for you
Sit upon your Father's lap
Hug Him in your heart
Listen to His heartbeat
Hear His words of life

OUR FATHER IN HEAVEN loves you beyond measure. He wants to give you every chance to have an even closer relationship with Him. To go higher and deeper into His heart and to have the mind of the Messiah.

To accomplish this, He intentionally sent Jesus who suffered, died and rose again for you. He is now seated at the Father's right hand, where you are also enabled to rest. Jesus is the High Priest and is the one who resides on the mercy-seat of your mind. He and Holy Spirit are the ones who bring revelation to you. You are saved to *live and move and have your being* in Jesus your High Priest. He is more valuable than all the valuables in the world. He died and suffered for you, and this reveals your worth. You are priceless and are one of His priests and kings.

As a son and daughter of Father God, you can build up a close relationship with Him. This is a relationship of greatest importance; the most valuable relationship of your life. It is in trusting, listening, conversing, believing, and partnering with Father God that you are able find favour and answers to your heart's cry and desire.

Joseph son of Jacob is a good example of someone who found favour:

> *The LORD made all that he did to succeed in his hand. And Joseph found favour in His sight, and he served him [Potiphar, the Egyptian master], and he made him an overseer.... And he put everything he had into his hand.*

> (Genesis 39:3)

Joseph had a good relationship with God as well as with his earthly father; he was Jacob's favourite son. God favoured Joseph. If you look at the word 'favour' it means: to be trusted and to be 'graced'. If God trusted Joseph, might He trust you? We can be confident that He trusts us as we follow our Fathers commands. We can do all things from a motivation of pleasing Father God.

Part of being a child of God is to focus on our spiritual selves. Our western culture has magnified the worth of the outward physicality of things. Jesus's king-domain shows us that the eternal value of life itself is within you and me. Our inner spiritual walk with God is everlasting, while the physical outer flesh is temporary.

Let us put the correct emphasis on our lives and be just as concerned about the spiritual as the physical. *'Seek first the kingdom of God and His righteousness, and all these* [physical] *things will be added to you'*. You are super valuable; trust Father God and His Son to look after you. In His Word, He gives instruction for you on how to be in the world; not to be part of its selfish focus.

You can focus on the inside and reside in heavenly realms where there is no lack. You can say with David, *'The LORD is my shepherd, I shall not want'*. You can soak in His presence in your rest times and be aware of Him filling you in your work times.

Jesus is your shepherd, and though fully God, he chose to be a human. He is interested in your natural state and has put in place physical acts you can do to enable you to move forward into the knowledge of who you are in Him.

Before He began His ministry, when He was around thirty years old, Jesus underwent a kind of transformation through being baptised. As Jesus was baptised by John, a kinsman, He heard Father God's audible voice saying, *'This is my beloved Son in whom I am well pleased'*. (Matthew 3:17). Father God wants to affirm your identity like this.

If you have not been baptised, this is a good reason to do so in order to know who you are in His kingdom. You are a son or daughter of God. This is part of the reason we need to be baptised, as it affirms our identity.

Baptism is a transformative act that is about purification; dying to your old life and becoming new in God. We are baptised into the name of Jesus and all that He has done for us. Just as children grow in the knowledge of who they are, so do we. Being baptised and receiving confirmation that you are a child of Father God is a beautiful gift.

A dove, which represented the Spirit of Adonai, descended on Jesus, modelling for us that after physical baptism, we are enabled to receive the Spirit of the Lord upon our life in a new way. Jesus wants to come upon you, as you humble yourself through baptism. If you are already baptised, Father God says to you this day: 'I am well pleased with you, beloved son, beloved daughter!'

Like Jesus each of us can be a son or daughter of our beloved Father. We are able, through faith and journeying with our Father and His Spirit, to be fully reflective of Jesus; to be like Him. One day soon, those who know the Father and the Son will be together fully betrothed to our Bridegroom, Priest and King; we shall be full of His glory.

Another aspect of being more like Him is being baptised into Holy Spirit which is celebrated every year at Pentecost. Shavuot, the Jewish feast falls on the same day. Shavuot was when Moses received the commandments and instructions from God on Sinai. If you have not done so already, ask the Holy Spirit to fill you and baptise you; ask for the gift of speaking in tongues and prophesy. I was baptised in this way in 1976 in a children's meeting and I prophesied. The gift of tongues came later and was more of a process for me, which was practiced over some years (I was 8 in 1976 so now you know how aged I am!). If you do not receive the gifts at first, keep having faith, relax and receive. Your Father will not give you a stone if you ask for bread.

The Spirit of the Lord has been sharing with me revelations concerning God being the Father of the bridegroom; we are betrothed to Jesus, His Son. God is also the father of the bride! Each of us are a part of His bride. Maybe this is the reason we wait for the return of our Messiah Jesus, so that everyone who is to be a part of the bride will be saved.

The Spirit of the Lord also talked with me concerning the fact that Jesus has been waiting a long time for His spotless bride, this encouraged me in waiting on Him during this time on earth. Let us spend time today in waiting on Him; you can be encouraged that your bridegroom knows how it feels to be human.

In Romans 8, it is written that Jesus was like us: '*He (God) sent His own Son in a likeness of sinful flesh*'. He can therefore identify with you in your suffering and while we wait for his return, we can also identify in His suffering. He still intercedes and feels for you, since He has gone through similar difficulties while living on earth. He has faith in you, that you will be able to overcome just as He did.

Many of us have been believing a lie that in order to be humble we should be seen as 'less than' or 'not worthy'; that we should not be 'great and marvellous' because that is prideful. However, many men and women who were truly great, such as Elijah the prophet, who rose up against the prophets of Jezebel; David, a shepherd boy, who slew the giant Goliath; Daniel and Joseph, who were known and moved in high governance; and Esther, who was called to be queen; were in positions of note and influence. All of them went through trials, testing and suffering. How much more can we overcome with the Spirit of the Lord both in us, as well as with us?

Where are these types of people in the gatherings of holy men and women today? Are you going ask the Lord for help to become one of these? We are called to greatness and at the same time to be humble. Confidence in God is not being prideful. You can be confident in God first and then in yourself, for He loves you immeasurably and has called you according to His purpose. Through you, He wants to do great exploits on earth in these days. We are to be humble and to *'be humbled under the mighty hand of God'*, so that He can lift us up. (1 Peter 5:6).

You are a child of the Most High God and a brother or sister to Jesus. If you have seen Jesus, you have seen and know the Father.

> *"To know me is to know my Father too. and from now on you will realise that you have seen him and experienced him."*

> (John 14:6-7 TPT)

I have known that I am a child of Father God more clearly since a vision I received in the early 2000s. I went to a conference at Revival Fires in Dudley, UK where we were worshipping in an elegant room with chandeliers and red seats rimmed in gold. Most of us left our seats and headed for the front where there was space to worship more freely. I had only recently learned to dance in worship at my home church and I proceeded to dance in what must have seemed a most ungainly manner due to my lack of dance practice.

The band were very much led by the Holy Spirit and during the lengthy time of magnifying our Lord, I went into an open vision of Jesus. I saw His face clearly. He was around thirty years old and He had shoulder-length hair and what I call a half-beard; a moustache and a little beard, but neatly trimmed. He had very kind eyes, which are what I remember most; His loving brown eyes (though I have also seen Him since with a light shining in His eyes, which seem a lighter colour due to this light).

In this open vision, I became a child of three years old and was stroking His face. It seemed to last a long time; just adoring Him as a child of Father God. Since this encounter I have never been the same, and I am very hungry to serve and to know Him more.

We can see ourselves and Jesus in the Bible. We have been and are being changed through the resurrection power of Jesus.

> *How beautiful on the mountains*
> *Are the sandaled feet of this one bringing such*
> *good news.*
> *You are truly royalty!*
> *The way you walk so gracefully in my ways*
> *Displays such dignity.*
> *You are truly the poetry of God – His very*
> *handiwork.*
> *Out of your innermost being*
> *Is flowing the fullness of my Spirit,*
> *Never failing to satisfy.*
> *Within your womb there is a birthing of*
> *harvest wheat;*
> *They are the sons and daughters nurtured by the*
> *purity you impart.*
> *How gracious you have become!*
> *Your life stands tall as a tower, like a shining light*
> *on a hill.*
> *Your revelation eyes are pure, like pools of*
> *refreshing – sparkling light for a multitude.*

(Song of Songs 7 TPT)

Father sees your heart first, before that which is on the temporal 'outside'. Your spiritual inner person is your heart. The encounters we have and the walk we have with our Father, Jesus, and Holy Spirit can transform our inner person, which in turn transforms our outer person. We desire to please Father God and not be disobedient; we desire to be more like Him.

Part of being a son and daughter is to have access to heaven and the hosts of heaven. Have you ever had a messenger from heaven visit you? It can happen at any time. I had such an encounter in 2005 after attending an impartation meeting where the whole church was prayed for, that our spiritual eyes would be open. Like Gahzi the servant of Elisha, my spiritual eyes were opened that evening after arriving back home. I was hungry for God after the service and was simply listening into the voice of God. I heard His voice within me saying, 'Go and kneel down and think about your Lord'. I was so hungry to experience Him, and I believe that hunger after God, and His righteousness, is a key to receiving all He has for you.

The preacher that night had said we were to *see* what the Father God was saying. He showed us how to concentrate on God with our eyes closed. To surrender our minds and imaginations to Him. We listened to some holy, peaceful instrumental music to help focus our minds and relax our bodies. We covered ourselves in the blood of Jesus and received sight from Holy Spirit. He told us to go home and practice hearing God and seeing visions in this way. Some refer to this as 'soaking in God's presence'.

Whilst praying after the meeting in my bedroom, the whole atmosphere was suddenly thick with an unexpected mighty presence. Warmth, love, and power radiated all around me. With my eyes closed, I was not able to move, and I was told: 'Do not be afraid'. I saw an angel who commissioned me saying, 'You are a priest of the Most High God'. While I was kneeling, the angel put into my left hand a brilliant orb of fire, which I was told to place into my heart. Disobedience wasn't an option! After this I stood and was given a branch or a rod in my right hand. The angel said, 'I will tell you when to strike with the rod'. After this the angel took me and we flew out through my bedroom window up into heaven where I enjoyed a special time with

Jesus. I believe such a solemn encounter can also be for you as a priest of the Most High. We can thank the Lord by faith for bringing us His messages to encourage us.

This experience reminded me of the text below and how we are clothed and made holy in Him. Put yourself into the picture of this scripture:

> *Then the angel showed me [and you] the priest standing before the angel of the Lord. Satan was standing at your right hand to oppose you . . . and the Lord God said to Satan, 'The Lord rebuke you! Is this [man or woman] not a brand saved from a fire? . . . Take off the filthy clothes'. . . . And turning to [you] he says, 'See, I have taken away your sins, and now I am giving you these fine new clothes'. . . This is what the Lord Almighty said to me: 'If you follow my ways and obey my requirements, then you will be given authority . . . I will let you walk in and out of my presence.'*

(Zechariah 3:17 NKJV)

The new clothes spoken of in Zechariah can bring the Lord's authority, His power, love and a sound mind; you are clothed in these as you encounter His presence in faith. Quite often I can see what my heart or inner spirit is wearing and Father clothes me with that which I need from heaven in order to give out to those who are in need on earth. It is through His 'mantle' and authority that you can bring supernatural help to others.

God will talk to you during many ways in your life. The main ways are by hearing, seeing and perceiving. As already mentioned, God may send His angel messengers. If you ask the Lord of hosts, our Father God, He may send you angel-messengers from his throne regarding particular requests. He is sovereign and loves to hear from you and I. Relax and listen to His still voice within you. Focus on God and Jesus; ask to be covered in Jesus' blood and surrender your heart and mind to them, then wait. Write down what you hear or see. Your Father has a good plan for you. Great things happen when we have faith in the Lord of the Angel Armies and are not afraid.

As any good teacher would, I encourage you to discern the angel messengers as you would anyone coming to your front door. Does it look like you can trust them? Do they have any identification (do they worship Jesus as Lord)? Satan knows the scripture but uses it to tempt or to question its validity. Angels of the Lord reflect Him and speak His words; they are good, kindly, righteous and just.

A part of our identity as kings and priests is to work with the angels whom Father God has made. Many of God's sons and daughters have worked with these pure spirits, who feature in the Bible on numerous occasions; warning people of danger, bringing good news and causing people to be placed in the right position or location which Father had ordained.

It is good to magnify and have faith in the Lord of the Angel Armies: YHVH *Tsavaot*. There are more godly angels than fallen ones, though the enemy's fallen ones have the ability to deceive us in thinking they have more authority and are more numerous and cause damage in our earthly realm for a limited time. Father God's army is huge and His power omniscient.

Worship is a key to being a son or daughter of The Most High. You are God's beloved to worship continually such as David did in the tabernacle of God. The name David means 'beloved'. In Acts 15, James speaks at the Jerusalem council and declares from the ancient biblical text that the Lord will 'rebuild the booth (or *sukkah*) of David' in the last days, so that all the gentiles will know the Lord (Amos 9:11). I believe that we are in the end-time period. This means that as a true worshipper you can worship the Father in the Spirit and in truth (John 4:23-24); you can tabernacle and worship Him in freedom.

We can worship the Lord our God with all our heart, mind, and body. It is all about giving our heart, soul and body to God as a living sacrifice in worship, so that out of love and adoration we desire to keep His commands, to follow His will, and to obey Him because we and He have a relationship of love. It is our voluntary love-sacrifice of worship to God.

This is what David's tabernacle or booth represents. We are kings and priests to serve Father God, just as David did. The worshipful elements of the lives of David, Solomon and Jesus show us what types of kings we can be; able to overcome evil through God's supernatural help, to be full of wisdom and able to see, do and bring about the will of the Father in heaven on earth.

Worship is a key to knowing who you are in God. Holy Spirit will cause you to experience tangible manifestations of God's kingdom. Many people are experiencing the phenomenon of gold being sent to them from heaven as they await our bridegroom to come and 'marry' us in covenant relationship forever. I had one such happening around 2006. We were standing and worshipping after having a talk about how Father God can manifest signs on earth from heaven. I had my Bible open in my hands as I was worshipping. My eyes were closed in singing worship for a little while. When I opened my eyes, there was a little heap of gold dust glimmering in the centre of my opened Bible. It was a wonder to behold! I now realise that it was a gift from my beloved Bridegroom. How wonderful!

One of the most beautiful aspects of the deeper things of the Lord has been that the Holy Spirit has given me a tune on my harp that is for me personally. I believe that everyone has a song in their hearts from Father God. Your Father God rejoices over you with singing (Zephaniah 3:17).

The more you humble yourself, submitting to the Word and Spirit, the more you realise you are a son/daughter in God's kingdom. This is a realisation which often takes time and process. However, in these days, the process is being accelerated. It says in the Bible that David became king of all Israel after reigning as king over his own tribe of Judah for seven years.

In a similar way, this sometimes happens with us. There may be a new beginning in our lives, such as starting a new job, and the process of learning this new role may take some time; it may involve tests, battles, and adventures. David was anointed as king as a young person and it took many battles and adventures for him to become ruler of all Israel. We too are also on this journey of moving into the role the Lord God has for each of us and it may take time and effort to receive the fullness of the good things of God.

There are some who think God is like people who sometimes fail us, or like an earthly father who was not always there for them or has let them down. Our Father is not like those people. He is holy, righteously perfect, just and full of powerful love. He invented love and has chosen love as His main attribute. He is continually choosing to love you!

We can know God's character more as we commune with Him. I have found in my communing and through His Word that the Holy Spirit has feminine attributes, like a mother. Father God, Holy Spirit and Jesus are all one. When you see one, you see all of them. God is mysterious, wonderful and awe inspiringly huge! God is your perfect mother and father figure, and if you have had lack on earth you can approach Him for help. Jesus quoted Psalm 118:

> *'how many times did I want to gather your children*
> *just as a hen gathers her brood under her wings'*

(Luke 13-34)

When I have needed a mother or fathers help and my natural parents could not help me, I have relied and depended on God, who was like a mother and father to me in my inner being and brought me peace and help when I needed it. God can bring healing where there is hurt and can protect you from further hurt. Ask and thank God for helping you. Conversely as you mature, you can be a mother or father to others who lack. After all you are becoming more like Him.

God's character is altogether perfect, and so you can trust Him/Them. You may not understand all Their ways. Their ways are above our ways and Their thoughts above ours (Isaiah 55:9). Any mistrust may be due to our own misunderstanding. Now is the time to ask for new understanding and knowledge of who God is. The easiest way to know more about God is to gaze and focus on Jesus the Messiah and to be continually filled with Holy Spirit. Jesus is humble and is not a proud ruler. He is a kind shepherd, king and priest. He is all in all.

Jesus is divine and you are made in His likeness. He is the Son of Man, fully like you, and has been tried and tested in all ways. He has known great pain and suffering in order that you can overcome the trials you face each day. He is your best example of how to rule and reign on the earth in love and mercy. He is the ruler of your life which you have been searching for. His ways are right and just. Ask Him to rule in your heart. Surrender your heart, mind, and body to His Word and to the trustworthy Holy Spirit.

> *For if we have become joined together in the likeness of His death, then we will also be united with the likeness of His resurrection . . .. In the same way, count yourselves to be dead indeed to sin, but living for God in Messiah Yeshua.*

> (Romans 6:5 & 11)

A good character in the Bible to study with regards your identity as king/queen is Esther. She typifies a queen who serves with a reigning king and who saves her nation through obedience to Mordecai her uncle and through wisdom. She is a type of 'Bride of Christ' in symbolic terms.

Queen Esther was willing to lay down her life to save her nation. She was full of courage and she fasted and prayed to ask God for a strategy about how to help her nation, who were about to be killed by her husband, the king. The king even broke one of his rules for her when she appeared before him uncalled; he gave her great favour by extending his sceptre to her.

Father God can do this for us as we enter into intimate relationship with Him more. Father loves faith in His subjects, He loves those made like Him. Like Esther, we can fast and pray together to ask Father God how we can release saving grace for our families, our friends, and the nations. Esther was prepared and anointed (as we are) for the task that God appointed for her to do, and she sought God vigorously for the lives of many who struggled with God.

You are a king/queen serving to bring God's kingdom to earth. The word of God shows us in pictorial form what the 'bride of Christ' looks like. Let us act upon and steward our lives according to the word of God.

You can thank your Father in heaven every day you were 'fearfully and wonderfully' made (Psalm 139). Even if you do not feel it, you can say in declaration: 'Marvellous are Your works, and my body knows right well'. You can ask: 'O God . . . lead me in *the way* everlasting!' *The Way* is mentioned many times in the Bible. Jesus says this (and you are made in His likeness): *'I am the way, the truth, and the life'.*

Above all, you are simply His beloved child. You are created by a loving Father who has millions of thoughts concerning you every day (Psalm 139). If you take time to reflect, you will see His hand guiding you, especially when you have taken time to pray and read His words of instruction throughout your life.

Prayer:

We humble ourselves under your hand and thank you that we are kings or queens by faith, who reign with you. Thank you that we are your sons and daughters whom you love very much. May you delight in us and us in you.

We thank You, Father God, for creating us and giving us life, for aligning us with Your destiny scroll in heaven; for our lives here on earth.

We plead the blood of the Lamb of God, who took away our sins, over our household and over all our destiny. We thank You for more of Your insight and revelation to show us who we are, where we are to be, and who we are to be with.

We worship you Father, thank you for all the parental help you have given. We receive all you have for our lives, in Your beloved Son's name.

Amen!

ELEVEN

You Are a House of Prayer

The Lamb of God's blood be over your soul
And heart, so that
The voice of the Lion of Judah can
With those of your tribe
Roar out His voice
Over our enemies!

YOU ARE A HOUSE OF PRAYER so that the nations and people can know what the love of Jesus looks like through your life. Communication with Father God, Jesus and Holy Spirit is a priority.

Continual communication with God is a joy throughout the day. Having a relationship with Him is the most important relationship of your life. Jesus took time alone communing with Father God in the mountains. Jesus went up higher in the natural, which reflects going up higher in the spiritual. Some of the best prayers are found in Bible passages, which you can use as prayers. Speaking these aloud to Father God is powerful.

The Psalms are a deep source of prayer to enable you to be honest and real with Father God. He loves you to be honest and to share how you are feeling whether jubilant or sad. He loves to have a joke as well as share deep and serious topics. For instance, I went through a season of talking with Him about all the different food we should have in the kingdom of heaven. He really is interested in what you think; He laughs at our funny ways.

The Word of God is a never-ending source and springboard of prayer for you. Prayer is basically any type of communication between you and God. Using His word as a foundation for your prayer is one of the most powerful ways to talk with God.

Below is a prayer, which the Father gave me from Colossians 4. Try reading Scripture aloud in your time with God and make it personal to you and others. This one is for you to pray in times of reaping the wonderful ripe harvest of souls. Holy Spirit showed this prayer to me as I was part of planning an outreach in London. I thank Father God for open doors for us and others to speak the mystery of the good news message of the Messiah, for this is what we are called to do.

Prayer:

I pray for open doors to speak the mysteries of the good news message of you, Messiah Jesus, to those in my sphere of influence. For this, Lord, is what you have asked me to do.

I pray that I would show the mystery of You Lord, when I speak out to others. Let me continually walk with wisdom toward those not yet part of Your Kingdom. Let me make the most of the time I have, to be able to do this as I go about life.

Let Your good news spill out of my life as I walk with Your grace. As I am seasoned with saltiness, let me know how to give a good answer to those I meet.

Amen and amen.

As discussed, our body is a temple of the Spirit of the Lord and as houses of prayer we are to be continually clean. I was watching a documentary recently about the Holy Land and the presenter spoke of when Jesus drove the money-changers out of the temple. As he was speaking, I had a godly thought in my heart. So often we let our bodies get cluttered with all sorts of wrong 'trading', just like those money changers. We spend our time and resources on the wrong things, such as bad movies, bad music, or bad news. This can clutter our lives with the wrong things. Jesus said, *"My Father's house shall be called a house of prayer for all nations, but you have made it a 'den of thieves'"* (Mark 11:17). We can ask Holy Spirit to search our hearts and we can repent and turn away from all bad 'trading'. How do we expect our Father to answer our prayers if we are not seeking to be righteous as He is righteous?

He wants us to be clean so we can be full of His glory, instead of being cluttered. Let us pray right now:

Thank you, Lord for cleansing me from all the clutter in my life. I repent and turn away from all evil, I ask your forgiveness and thank you for your supernatural cleansing.

Thank you for your powerful blood Jesus which makes me white as snow.

Fill me up Spirit of the Lord that I may a delight to you!

Amen.

We are collectively a 'House of Prayer' and we need each other. All together we are one and we are the fullness of the Messiah on earth: the *ekklesia,* which is translated as 'church' in many versions of the Bible. This word means 'faithful gathering'. One of the reasons that we gather faithfully together is to pray. Prayer is more powerful and effective as we pray in unity. It is written that one will send a thousand to flight (in terms of enemy action), and two will send ten thousand. This implies that two are ten times more effective in their agreements with Father God than one person alone. Let us pray together regularly to further the kingdom of heaven on earth.

By being in relationship and submitting your life to Jesus and by being accountable to each other, you will have the power and the '*strength of His might which He brought about in Messiah when He raised Him from the dead*'. (Ephesians 1:19-20). Together we stand in His power.

One of the keys to receiving the might and power of the Lord is to thank Him for forgiving our disobedience to the instructions of Father God. We can repent and obey the commands He has given in the scriptures. I recently had a vision of Jesus covered in his prayer shawl. He focused in on the tassels at the end of the shawl He wore. Afterward, I researched the meaning of these and found that Father God gave this command to Israel which I have personalised for this quote:

> *Make fringes for yourselves in the wings (corners)*
> *of your garments throughout your generations and*
> *that you put upon the fringe of the border a thread*
> *of blue . . . and it will be to you a fringe, that you*
> *may look on it and remember all the commands*
> *of the Lord and do them, and that you do not seek*
> *after your own heart and your own eyes . . . so you*
> *will remember and do all my commands and be*
> *holy to your God. I am the Lord your God who*
> *bought you bought you out of Egypt (the world), to*
> *be your God: I AM the Lord your God'*

(Numbers 15:38-40)

Father God's commands are for our benefit to live in community together in His peace. The main part of our prayer life is to remember His instruction to love Him and each other with the love He has put in our hearts. I pray that Holy Spirit will continue to remind you of the right way to live and that you would be full of grace to be able to live in good community with each other daily.

One more prayer Holy Spirit has taught me is out of Philippians 4. Paul urges us to *'Be in agreement in the Lord'*. It appears that Euodia (meaning 'prosperity') and Syntyche (meaning 'fortunate') disagreed over something. Paul writes that these two names are written in the 'scroll of life', as if to say these two are holy and need to agree. He asks others to help them and then goes on to exhort everyone to *'rejoice in the Lord always . . . Your gentleness must be known to all people. The Lord is near'*. Paul says that as we quickly let our requests be known to God and thank Him, God's very peace will keep us focused on Jesus our Messiah.

Prayer:

Thank You, Lord, for helping us to agree with those who are our brothers and sisters in you, especially those who we find a challenge, whose names are written in heaven's books.

For those in disagreement today, we pray that they would get the help they need to find your peace together.

We pray for unity among us, and for your empathy and peace.

We receive more of your gentleness and enablement to give to others, and your joy for strength to maintain everything good we receive from you.

We give you our worries and fears right now and receive your peace instead. Thank You Lord, for new and continual focus on you and on all that is right and good.

Amen.

Another prayer which the Holy Spirit recently gave me for you to pray was as I worked on our company accounts. I was typing away and the Holy Spirit told me, 'Breathe!' I thought I had been breathing but He meant for me to breathe deeply. This led into a prayer time in which I was shown to pray for my family to be full of the breath of God; to be covered by the blood of Jesus and to receive hearing and sight from Lord. These aspects were the very aspects of God indwelling in me and you. He was asking me to pray the prayer of John 17, where Jesus asked for us *'to be one as I am one with you Father'*.

Prayer:

I surrender my all to You, Lord God.
I receive Your breath Spirit of the Lord.
I receive Your cleansing, transforming blood in and over me.
I receive Your mindset Lord Jesus.
I receive Your hearing and I receive Your sight.
I ask for your blood covering over myself and my family.
Thank You for filling us all with Your love.

Amen.

Finally, I wanted to encourage you to speak and search out deep prayers in the Bible. Go deeper. Jesus, your beloved, loves you very much, and He wants to you to grow exponentially in your faith. In His Word there are many mysteries to be mined. One of those is found in the Song of Songs:

> *Why would you [brides-to-be] want to see my dance of love? Because you dance so gracefully, as though you danced with angels.*

> (Song of Songs 6:12-13 TPT)

The Hebrew word for this 'dance with angels' is '*mahanaim*', and it is first mentioned in Genesis 32:12. When Jacob returned to the promised land, he entered at this actual place, the name of which means 'dance of two camps'. Having researched this, I found that Jewish messianic perspective speaks of these camps as the place where the human army of the Lord (the bride of Christ) meets with the angelic army of the Lord, to worship in dance. Could this dance be a dance of war; a dance of victory over our enemies?

We can rejoice and dance in faith. This is for both men and women. The armies in biblical times always went out in worship before battle and many of the dancers would have been men. There is something about using your whole body as a living sacrifice to the Lord which is powerful. I encourage you to lift up your head and arms to the Lord and bow before Him in worship – these things are a type of simple dance movement before Him. I have inquired of the Lord concerning this, and I pray the following:

Prayer:

I come before You as part of Your great army; Your soldier bride. I come before You, my bridegroom Jesus.

Lord, I would love to come to the place of the 'dance of the *mahanaim*' in my spiritual life so that I can join the 'dance of the two camps' giving my body as a living spiritual sacrifice to You.

I join with Your angel armies so that I can show my bridegroom how much I love Him. Thank you that as I look to You, I am even more powerfully equipped to share Your good news to those who are lost and to enforce the victory You have already won.

Thank you for this place of two camps where heaven meets earth. I pray that as I 'dance' through this life in Your Spirit, angelic hosts from heaven's armies go out to enforce Your will be done on earth; enforcing love, joy and harmony to reign and wickedness to flee.

Thank you, Lord of the angel armies, that You are the gateway for heaven to invade earth.

Amen.

As an aside, the word 'amen' originates in the Hebrew word for faith which is 'emonah'. When you say 'amen' you are agreeing in faith with that which is spoken. Faith-filled words are powerful and creative.

No chapter on prayer would be complete without the Lords' Prayer, which I most regularly pray when I visit patients in hospital as part of our local chaplaincy team. Most mature patients know this powerful prayer by heart, and it is a great comfort to many, especially those with early dementia. Even after many years they always remember the words. I have heard a testimony in which a man who was dying said the Lords' prayer, having been taught it by his grandma. He credits the prayer with him being delivered from death, earning him precious years with his family. I wanted to write the prayer as it is written on my heart (and not quote directly from written text) for it is in our hearts where the Bible causes our lives to flourish:

Our Father who is in Heaven,
Holy is Your name,
May Your kingdom come,
May Your will be done,
On earth, as it is in heavenlies
(where there is no sin, sickness nor evil effect)
Lead us not into temptation,
And deliver us from all that is evil,
For Yours is the kingdom,
The power and the glory.
Forever and ever,
So be it.

TWELVE

Who I Am, a Testimony

AFTER READING PSALM 139

From your mother's womb
Till the tomb of flesh
Through His cross
To resurrection birth
Womb of your second start
And back to your Father's heart

IF YOU DO NOT FULLY KNOW JESUS yet and desire him to reside in your heart continually, read this testimony and pray the prayer at the end.

If you have walked some time with Jesus and are like Him, then writing out your own testimony is one way of finding out who you are. As you look back, you can see how far you have come; you can see more aspects of how Father God has encouraged you to grow. Write your testimony down even if you do not want to make it public. This discipline will help you share it with others more clearly and be a great encouragement through trials. You will see just how far you have come.

Here is mine.

A Butterfly Life Story

Some species of butterfly fly a three-thousand-mile journey. Some, like the monarch butterfly, begin their journey high in the mountains. Moses, Jesus and other prophets used to go up onto the high mountains to pray to Father God for direction. We can also go into His realm in our devotional time. You and I are on the journey of life.

Butterflies are mature insects; they have come of age. If we find God, then I believe we must endeavour to 'come of age' and be mature in our faith in who he is and who we are.

God created the African swallowtail with little mirror-like sections within their wings which allow them to glow brightly in darkness. Scientists have relatively recently invented Light Emitting Diodes (LEDs) based on these butterflies.

Allow the struggle of life, the chrysalis of love, to mature you so that you have wings to fly above and see things differently. Drink the nectar of the Holy Spirit, who is full of peace and joy, to give you strength.

When I was a baby, my mother prayed and cried out to God over my cot, even though she did not know Him that well. She prayed that I would have a better life than her. God listened to her cry. When I was growing up, I had a deep sense of eternity in my heart and from a young age was drawn to God.

My caterpillar life of knowing God began in Fleet, Hampshire. My father was away working long hours. My mother was in a bad way at that time and was on suicide watch with the local doctor. Mum was very depressed, and her life would have fallen apart severely were it not for her finding out about God and giving her life over to Him.

Our good friend Pam Robertson helped Mum follow Jesus and she showed Mum how she could have power to overcome. Mum went from smoking sixty cigarettes a day to none in one day – a miracle! As an eight-year-old, I saw Mum change dramatically from a drink-swilling, smoke-filled depressive, to a shiny, flourishing and happy woman.

In line with her, I too began to change and became a leaf-munching, Bible-reading, Jesus-singing, faith-speaking, caterpillar Christian.

I talked a lot about God, and I tried excitedly to show my friends about my faith. This was not welcomed in most cases and I became an outcast caterpillar Christian among the girls at Courtmoor junior school. Being a very shy child, this did not help with social learning skills, since being a Christian was not a popular pastime.

One of my friends was Marion Crofts, who became my best friend at senior school. I shared lots about my growing faith with Marion.

God has protected and used me amazingly throughout my life. For example, Marion and I were close friends in the first two years of senior school, cycling to school together every day and meeting up after school. In the second year of senior school, my dad decided to move our family to Farnborough. We did not quite realise why God allowed us to sell our house so easily in a bad housing market (Dad did not use an estate agency). We all prayed as a family one day: 'Lord if you want us to move to Farnborough, to the house Dad feels we should have, then sell our Fleet house today, Lord'. That very day, an Indian man sat on our sofa and purchased our house for cash.

I had been at my new school and was missing my old friends, especially Marion, though we kept in touch by mail. We had moved in the autumn but by June of the next year we received a huge shock. Marion was murdered brutally, and the story was covered on national media. Many friends and family were affected by this tragedy. I am glad I had the privilege of knowing Marion and I have the assurance that she is currently in heaven.

I now know that God took me out of the situation of being at Courtmoor School to enable me to carry on with my life relatively unscathed from the effects of the brutal murder of my best friend. He protected me from the emotional effects. Yes, I was questioned by the police; yes, I shed lots of tears; but I was taken out of the heavy atmosphere of grief which was apparent at Courtmoor. Being sensitive, perhaps I was taken out of there as God knew that I would not have fared well.

However, my relationship with my God grew in wisdom and I grew a little bit taller. I was still a very shy caterpillar as a teenager, so I sought to overcome this problem myself by traveling and working hard to better myself.

I ended up working in Dad's business, where I became so much more confident and felt I wanted to do a degree and be something or someone more. Looking back, I can see I tried too hard by myself and was not leaning on Father God all the time.

I chose to go to a small college in Chichester to do my degree in English creative writing and Religious Studies. I think I chose a small college because I was afraid I would not be able to cope in the city. This may have been an unwise choice. Never choose a direction based on fear. Go with your heart and with what God is saying.

I was a born again, Bible-believing, all-singing caterpillar Christian, put into a room next to a white witch on one side, an atheist on the other, and an agnostic downstairs.

Being an innocent pure white caterpillar, I found it difficult to remain with God amid the stinky rubbish of college life. Within three years, I graduated not only with a good degree in English and Religious Studies, but also graduated from cider to Guinness, having hardly touched alcohol before.

In many ways, I was not wise at college and I gradually became hardened toward the things of God. I was not eating from the Bible but rubbish for my supper every day. I soon grew very thin and I kept having accidents, ending up on crutches due to drinking too much; my third accident in a year and a half. Looking back, the course I chose also had a detrimental effect on my life as I was studying all the religions of the world. This meant visiting temples, chanting mantras and reading sutras which were not of my own faith.

My faith was tested in all areas and I chose not to meditate on the Word of God nor regularly worship with His people. Still, God did not neglect me and looked after his little caterpillar.

When I came home during holidays and weekends, I attended our local church. I became close friends with Matt, my future husband, at a church barbecue. My handsome hero and I became engaged at a Valentine's Ball, though neither of us were very close to God. We split up quite badly for eight months during which time I became closer to God once more and again became a healthier caterpillar Christian. I leaned on God and worshipped Him in the pain of separation. I think this was a pain-filled pupa moment!

From then on, my life was in the struggling stage of chrysalis. Matt and I married, now my best friend, in an amazing wedding in 1995. Our wedding was a prophecy of things to come: everyone was invited, and it was generous and full of music, love and life. It was abundant and we both saw to it that it was a beautiful bug ball.

Work life was difficult in lots of ways for me and real struggle, but finally I found a great company to work with and was paid well. Matt had an excellent career and we set up home and had a good lifestyle. However, I was still relatively fearful and shy of others. This fear of man has, by faith and deliverance, all but disappeared now that I am in the jubilee of life. One of the keys to overcoming has been to seek the Lord, His kingdom realm, His righteousness and truth with all my heart, soul and strength. It is through the love of our Father, His Son's sacrifice and in-filling of Holy Spirit that I have been and am being set free. I am a new creation; old things have passed away and a new day has begun. I would say that one of the keys to being close to God has been through daily Bible meditation, worship and prayer.

Butterfly Moments

I can look back at times which were the first appearing of a butterfly from the pupa; giving birth and having kids, and a number of experiences and encounters with God some of which are outlined above. We had two wonderful children by 2004.

One of my butterfly moments happened when we were in church, and our minister put on a soundtrack from a song and asked us to stand and 'drink in' God's presence. At the time I was worried about our finances since Matt was due to leave our main source of income and set up a business, with me as finance co-ordinator. It was a gamble and for the first time in our lives we were taking a big risk; having a big mortgage and car loans to pay for by faith. We were relying on God to help us win new jobs to create our own income.

For the second time in my life I was bought to my knees by God in a dramatic way. I wept, mainly grieving at my own lack of faith for the task ahead and cried out to God: 'Father, Father, please forgive us!' again and again. It was as if I were crying for the whole church as well as our lives. I was changed completely after this experience, it felt like heart surgery; I could never be the same again.

When I stood up and dried my eyes, I became more confident of who I was. I knew God had forgiven me, he had given me a gift of faith and I knew His power on my life. My confession was different, I was changed, and the feelings of anxiety were gone. I was not worried about finances; in fact, I spoke to others about looking forward to being successful. Today we run a successful business. I believe one of the keys was that I was vulnerable and prepared to cry out to the Lord and he heard the cry of my heart. We read of such emotions in the Psalms: *'I cried to the Lord and He delivered me from all my fears'* (Psalm 34:4).

Another butterfly moment happened when as a family we went to Israel in 2015 where, on the Mount of Transfiguration, a big yellow swallowtail butterfly landed on my finger. I knew that my Father loved me and is transforming me in spirit, soul, and body. It was a significant moment because before this time God had talked to me about transformation of my life through butterflies several times. In fact, I wrote this testimony before the swallowtail landed on my hand. I feel as if I now have wings to fly above the worldly doom and gloom. With Holy Spirit in me, I am on a journey of more than three thousand miles and I am learning to receive and release more of my Creator's power, faith, love, and hope. I am moving up to the mountain top of my life here on earth. I am laying down many seeds, from the hand of God, which will produce an inheritance for His kingdom; for His glory.

You have such a hope in Him. You can know that your future with God is better than anything you can imagine or understand. One day your identity will be fully integrated into His when Jesus returns. As promised in the book of Revelation, you will see Him as he really is when the natural and supernatural converge. Presently, you have the Holy

Spirit's help to show you more fully the extent of the love Father God has for you *in*, and because of, His son. You will know who He is making you to be. The Apostle John writes:

> *'Beloved, now we are children of God; and it has not yet been revealed what we shall be, but we know that when He is revealed, we shall be like Him, for we shall see Him as he is'*

(1 John 3-2)

What a great hope we have in Jesus our Messiah, our hope of glory.

I would like to end this chapter with a short poem and prayer for you.

Altogether holy

Not only good
not only right
but altogether holy
in His sight

Good fear of the Lord
light so bright
casts out Fears
chases out fright

Not just good
and not just right
but altogether holy
in His sight

Like a tree of bad
my life grew both
so I grew sad

He hung on the bad
so the tree did die
And I saw His face
and we rose again

He planted me a seed
it was a tree of life
His root grew deep
now His branch am I

Flowers unfurled
leaves uncurled
Much fruit grown
I watch Him smile

He's not only good
He's not only right
but He's altogether holy
in my sight.

Prayer:

Here is a prayer to say from your heart to His:

Lord Jesus, Your name means Saviour.

I need saving!

I surrender my whole self to You; body, mind, and spirit.

Thank You for forgiving me of all disobedience, the lies and anything which is against Your commands. I do not want to do anything that displeases You again.

I am made in the likeness of You, and I want to do the right thing, like You do. I want to focus on all that is good and right.

Holy Spirit come into my heart and clean me out. Turn my life around and make me a new person; the person You always made me to be. Give me the wings of Your Spirit to fly high like Psalm 103 says: *'you have supercharged my life so that I soar again like a flying eagle in the sky!'* (TPT). Thank You that I am transformed into your new creation.

Thank You for making me like You and filling me with Your goodness and kindness continually; with Your love everlasting.

Thank You for saving me from all evil and leading me to know the Father's heart for my life.

Thank You that my name is in Your book of life.

Amen.

Final Thoughts

I trust these pages have helped show you something more of who you are in Jesus; of how to be closer to Father God and how to go deeper into the experience of His great love for you. Thank you for sharing this journey with me into identity and what it means in the context of His Word and Spirit.

My hope is that you have been encouraged in your faith, that your faith in Father God, in Jesus and Holy Spirit has grown as you have listened to the testimony within these pages.

To know the Lord Jesus and Father God in the Spirit is the mainstay of life and the more you know them, the more you will be like them.

May you learn to love and live more like Him and at the end may your name be in His heavenly everlasting book.

> *'May our Father in heaven give you the Spirit of Wisdom and revelation so that you may know Him better.'*

(Ephesians 1:17)

After finishing this book, I was asked by our mission leader to read Bill Johnsons book 'Hosting His Presence' which resonates with the premise of this entire book. Bill writes: 'our true nature and personality will never come into fullness apart from His manifest presence. Like Him – personality and function.'[1]

There is so much more to being Like Him, for instance, Jesus as your shepherd King, great counsellor, miracle maker, teacher and prophet. Even if all the books in all the world could not contain the extent of His glorious 'Being'. One thing I do know; His likeness is beautiful, let us seek Him more.

> *'One thing have I desired of the LORD, that will I seek after; that I may dwell in the house of the LORD all the days of my life, to behold the beauty of the LORD, and to enquire in His temple.'*

(Psalm 27:4 KJV)

When we find Him in our daily lives, being continually aware of the Lord's presence; we desire to delight Him. We desire to enforce the victory over sin, death and hell which He has already won. Being like Him will cause us to be His living habitations. His Holy Word has gone forth and it is now time for us to spiritually act upon it, for as He is generous and so therefore are we.

---

1. Hosting the Presence, Bill Johnson, 2013, Destiny Image